THE POWER OF PROCOVERY

IN HEALING MENTAL ILLNESS

Just Start Anywhere

Kathleen Crowley

Courtesy of Kennedy Carlisle Publishing Co. for Health Action Network, Inc.
San Francisco, California

With grateful appreciation for the support of the State of Wisconsin
Division of Supportive Living and the Milwaukee County Department
of Human Services, Mental Health Division

Kennedy Carlisle Publishing Co.

P.O. Box 2247

San Francisco, CA 94126

The Power of Procovery in Healing Mental Illness: Just Start Anywhere

Profits from the sale of this book support the Health Action Network, a 501(c)(3) non-profit organization aimed at empowering individuals in health care. Contact us at act4health@aol.com or www.procovery.com.

The ideas and suggestions in this book are not intended as medical or psychological advice, and are for informational and educational purposes only. Anyone who experiences serious mental illness needs to be under the care of expert health care professionals. Serious mental illness is dangerous and can be life threatening. The treatment strategies described in this book do not replace on-going treatment. Do not abruptly stop other treatments in deference to the ones described in this book. Modify your treatment only after you have carefully considered and discussed it with trusted health care professionals, and have put appropriate monitoring and support systems in place.

First Edition

ISBN: 0-9643348-2-8

Printed and bound in the United States of America.

TABLE OF CONTENTS

A Note to the Reader

"The way a book is read—which is to say, the qualities a reader brings to a book—can have as much to do with its worth as anything the author puts into it."
—Norman Cousins

Marshall McLuhan wrote, "the medium is the message." This book seeks in its design to illustrate the principles and power of procovery.

First, as you read this book, you will find that one of the chief strategies for procovery is to just start anywhere, and move forward in any increment. This book operates on the same principle. Read the chapters at any time, in any order; or just pick up the book from time to time for a quote, an anecdote, or an idea.

Second, the essence of procovery is that ordinary, practical steps can be of enormous healing consequence. So each chapter on a procovery strategy is followed by "Procovery Notes"—ideas and tips you might implement *today*.

Third, procovery is about what all individuals—consumers, family, and staff—can do despite the limitations of symptoms and systems. So the procovery notes are written separately for each group of readers: "Procovery Notes for Consumers," "Procovery Notes for Family Members," and "Procovery Notes for Staff."

This book is intended to be a living book, accompanied by

a web site www.procovery.com. Procovery is a healing approach by and for individuals. We would love you to contribute to the web site your individual stories and experiences about what works (and doesn't) for you, and help others procover.

Foreword

Kathleen Crowley has done what few writers in the mental health field can do or have done. Kathleen has combined her personal experience of the mental health system, her own remarkable insights, and the life experience of others to fashion a highly readable and informative book. *The Power of Procovery* is designed to help people diagnosed with severe mental illness create more meaningful and fulfilling lives, i.e., to help bring about procovery.

Kathleen's concept of procovery implies that people diagnosed with severe and chronic mental illness can take control of their lives and become healed. One must not fall into the trap of waiting passively for the caregiver to come up with the solution or cure. Procovery focuses on what the person with the diagnosis can do to take action—to move forward with one's life—and how family and treatment staff can be more helpful in supporting procovery.

The Power of Procovery is a treasury of strategies about how to become the person one wants to be, in spite of once being diagnosed with severe mental illness. Consistent with the theme of procovery the book is designed so the reader has the choice about where to begin the book! According to Kathleen procovery does not have only one starting point or one ending point. Treat the book accordingly. Scan the Table of Contents and choose the topic with which you wish to start.

For example, at the beginning of *The Power of Procovery* Kathleen helps you turn the diagnostic process into an opportunity to begin the healing process. Kathleen gives the person diagnosed a number of ways to take control of the diagnosis, rather than letting the diagnosis control the person. In the book's Notes to Family & Staff there are insights into how to help make the diagnostic process, which is too often a dehumanizing experience, into a hopeful time.

But you may not start the book at the beginning! As Kathleen implores in the book's subtitle—*Just Start Anywhere*. Perhaps you want to create a better partnership between caregiver and consumer, or develop sound medication management strategies, or learn to become more hopeful again, etc. Start reading *The Power of Procovery* at the chapter heading that appears most relevant to your current experience. There are so many ideas that some will fit for you right now.

If you are a family member or staff member pay special attention to the book's Notes section directed specifically at you. *The Power of Procovery* is inspiring for staff and family as well as consumers. If staff and family members incorporate the strategies compatible with the procovery philosophy, the chances improve that the consumer's procovery path will be smoother, straighter, and contain fewer obstacles.

The Power of Procovery is must reading for all in the mental health field. Anecdotes, metaphors and quotations combine to make Kathleen's writing jump off the page and sink into your heart. Kathleen values the reader's time, and conveys her ideas eloquently and succinctly. The writing and the format invite the reader to read *The Power of Procovery* all in one sitting, but it is a book meant to be read in bits and pieces. And to be re-read when certain topics become most relevant in one's unique journey toward procovery. Keep this valuable book close-by. There are many gems in these pages. Your life will be richer for reading and using *The Power of Procovery*.

—William A. Anthony, Ph.D.
    Executive Director & Professor
    Boston University Center for Psychiatric Rehabilitation

Procovery and the New Millennium

Sinikka McCabe, Administrator
Division of Supportive Living
Wisconsin Department of Health and Family Services

Kathleen Crowley's book, *The Power of Procovery in Healing Mental Illness—Just Start Anywhere* meets a critical need in the mental health field as this field enters the new century and millennium. Over the past decade, the public mental health system has embraced the concept of recovery that brings hope to individuals with mental illness, their families, the provider community as well as policy makers and funders. However, implementing a concept in one's day-to-day life or practice requires a great deal of knowledge and practical advice.

Kathleen Crowley has combined her personal knowledge and experience in the mental health system in this wonderful book that meets the amazing challenge of providing guidance and very practical advice to consumers, families and providers all in one book!

The great value of this book is in its ability to take the new and revolutionary concept of recovery and make it understandable and applicable to a wide group of readers. The book can and should be considered a teaching tool and reference book for consumers and practitioners alike.

In Wisconsin, the public mental health system has made a very clear commitment to implement recovery concepts across the system. Kathleen's book will be of great value in making this vision a reality. In fact, Kathleen was one of the key persons in designing the blue print for Wisconsin public mental health system reform and we are now very lucky to have her insight on how to implement this concept.

Another perhaps even more important aspect of this book is the gentle but relentless, all permeating sense of hope that Kathleen weaves into every chapter and every paragraph of the book. Her belief in each individual's ability to work toward attaining a productive and fulfilling life regardless of the level of health is a powerful vision that leaves the reader deeply moved and changed in his/her perception about the ability of persons with mental illness to get better. The quotes so eloquently used in the book leave the reader moved and greatly hopeful for the future.

Finally, the book's friendly format—just start anywhere—invites the reader to pick up the book, select a chapter of most interest and start reading and applying. The just start anywhere philosophy also comes through in Kathleen's concept of procovery: there are numerous possibilities as to where to start the procovery process in each person's life. The hope and positive belief of just starting anywhere does not go unnoticed as one reads through the book.

Much too long in the public mental health system have we settled for maintenance of the people we serve and status quo in the system. *The Power of Procovery* provides us a challenge to look at our services, approaches and methods in delivering services. It gives us the vision, the hope as well as concrete ideas on how to do this. Let's follow Kathleen's advice and start anywhere and everywhere in applying hope and practical strategies in making procovery a reality for everyone in our service systems!

To fight aloud is very brave,

But gallanter, I know,

Who charge within the bosom,

The cavalry of woe.

Who win and nations do not see,

Who fall, and none observe,

Whose dying eyes, no country,

Regards with patriot love.

We trust, in plumed procession,

For such the angels go,

Rank after rank, with even feet

And uniforms of snow.

—Emily Dickinson

Power of Procovery

The voyage of discovery lies not in finding new landscapes but in having new eyes. —Marcel Proust

The concept of procovery is so simple, so available, and so rooted in common sense it's almost funny that it took me years to get a glimpse of it, years to grasp the fundamentals. Namely: Sometimes healing has little to do with health; sometimes recovery in the traditional sense is not an option; and often we need to rewrite the scripts of our lives and reach forward to the largely unknown rather than backward to the familiar.

The fundamental focus of procovery is one of moving forward when you can no longer move back, of letting go of what was and rebuilding new dreams. Of accepting the realities of illness while focusing on life. Procovery offers individuals diagnosed with psychiatric disorders an approach to attaining a productive and fulfilling life, regardless of the level of health assumed attainable.

William Anthony, Ph.D., executive director of the Center for Psychiatric Rehabilitation at Boston University, writes that efforts to help sufferers of severe mental illness can not only leave a person less impaired, less disabled, and less disadvantaged, but leave a person "with more—more meaning, more purpose, more success, and more satisfaction with one's life."[1]

This book is designed to offer *more*, to offer concrete, practical information for consumers, staff, and family as to how to bring about procovery; and to show that individuals can do so regardless of the limitations of systems and symptoms.

I learned about the power of procovery personally years ago, through a slew of hit-and-miss propositions, that only in hindsight did I recognize as a path forward.

Opening the Door to Procovery

One cannot get through life without pain. . . . What we can do is choose how to use the pain life presents to us.
—Bernie Siegel, M.D

For years I was convinced that my problem—clinical depression accompanying chronic pain—was medical. I thought that once "they" diagnosed the problem and treated the problem, "they" would cure the problem. I felt that nothing short of returning to life as I'd known it was acceptable. I thought that I needed a simple three-step program: 1) find the right doctor; 2) have him run the right tests; 3) be prescribed the right treatment.

Then one day at UCLA (where I was being treated at the time), I was told that they probably would not be able to reduce the physical pain I was experiencing, which they likened to that of someone with terminal cancer. And that as chronic pain and depression so often go hand in hand, I would likely be battling both for life.

But then, "We do have some good news, though," I heard someone say. I remember trying to reach through the fog, the busy stream of thoughts running through my mind. They have good news, I thought. Thank God.

"We feel that while we may be unable to affect the actual level of pain you are experiencing, Kathleen, we may be able to teach you to reduce the *bothersomeness* of it." I was then abruptly sent back to the psychiatric ward, in a daze, trying to fathom this.

It struck me as inconceivable that I could live every day in pain, physical and emotional, and learn to function again. No one had even suggested at that point that I would learn to be productive or happy again. Just that I might learn to survive.

The escort assigned to walk me back was one I'd been assigned several times before, a nice guy, a student at UCLA. I decided I would run all of this by him. The suicidal depression . . . the pain comparable to that of someone with terminal cancer . . . nothing they could do . . . battling both for life . . . good news . . . possibility I can learn to reduce the *bothersomeness* of it?

He stopped dead in his tracks as we were walking. "They said that to you?" he asked. And then after a long pause, and somewhat under his breath, he said, "Wow, and you're the one locked in the psychiatric ward."

My sentiments exactly, I thought.

How could I survive in constant physical and emotional pain? How could I care for my two precious daughters? How could my husband continue to love me when all he really wanted was for me to "be the way you used to be"? How, at the age of 27, could I make a life for myself that resembled nothing of the life I'd dreamed of and mapped out? How, when all my dreams were now impossible, could I go on?

But here I am, over 15 years later, writing this book, to tell you what I ultimately found absolutely shocking. *They were right.* I have been able to reduce the bothersomeness of both my pain and my depression. I am today not cured but healed.

We all have enormous power to help ourselves and others procover. And that is what this book is all about.

What is Procovery?

Procovery / n: attaining a productive and fulfilling life regardless of the level of health assumed attainable [vs. recovery, returning to a prior state of health]

The focus is not to do remarkable things but to do ordinary things with the conviction of their immense importance.
—Teilhard de Chardin

Procovery is an approach to healing based on hope and grounded in practical everyday steps that individuals can take to move forward.

More specifically, procovery addresses the question, "When I can't move backward, in the traditional sense of recovery, what can I do?" with the answer that individuals can:

- Move forward

- Through individual actions

- That are ordinary,

- Regardless of the limitations of systems and symptoms, and

- With faith in the possibilities, even though the path may be difficult and indirect.

Changing the focus from reaching backward to moving forward can rebalance the scale by which we measure our lives. Focusing on *defeating* chronic illness often will result in losses that appear to vastly exceed gains—where life without illness will not be regained, and a hellish life of striving to cope remains.

This has to do with what Erich Fromm[2] describes in *The Sane Society* as "the whole 'balance' concept of life as an enterprise which can fail. Many cases of suicide are caused by the feeling that 'life has been a failure,' that 'it is not worthwhile living any more'; one commits suicide just as a businessman declares his bankruptcy when losses exceed gains, and when there is no more hope of recuperating the losses."

Focusing on *overcoming* chronic illness, on integrating illness into life, shifts the balance—although illness is one *specific* loss, it no longer dominates the equation, and the future holds potential.

In an essay called "Lessons from the Art of Surgery," Richard Selzer, a surgeon, writes eloquently of the meaning of letting go of what was and embracing what can be:

> The young woman speaks. 'Will my mouth always be like this?' she asks.
>
> 'Yes,' I say, 'it will. It is because the nerve was cut.'
>
> She nods, and is silent. But the young man smiles.
>
> 'I like it,' he says. 'It is kind of cute.'
>
> All at once I know who he is. I understand, and I lower my gaze. One is not bold in an encounter with a god. Unmindful, he bends to kiss her crooked mouth, and I so close I can see how he twists his own lips to accommodate to hers, to show her that their kiss still works. I remember that the gods appeared in ancient Greece as mortals, and I hold my breath and let the wonder in.

Procovery is built upon the idea that each person's path is unique, that idiosyncrasies are the soul and not the bane of healing, and that inflexible task lists and expectations often condemn and imprison rather than heal.

This essential individuality of procovery has two important

consequences. First, different individuals start procovering in different places and along entirely unique paths, so procovery utilizes a "just start anywhere" philosophy—individuals can begin anywhere in any increment. Item 4 on the task list need not necessarily be completed before item 5. For each of us, as Rachel Naomi Remen, M.D., writes, there are "conditions of healing that are as unique as a fingerprint."

Second, because procovery is an individual path it will not "look" the same for any two individuals—or even for the same individual over time. As C.B. Keogh notes in one of the GROW handbooks, "The line between sickness and health must be drawn through the center of each person rather than be used by one group to separate itself from another."[3]

Procovery is also built upon the ordinary. Jay Neugeboren, whose brother Robert has spent most of his life, since the age of 19, in hospitals and psychiatric wards around New York City, writes of the time and money spent searching for organic causes and cures, "while back on the ward patients languish and die for the simple lack of human attention to their ordinary, daily needs."[4] It is often thought that big problems need big solutions. In fact, small steps can carry great distances.

Procovery is both an end and a means, a destination and a process of getting there. It is not a *model* of medicine or rehabilitation, not a replacement for pharmaceutical treatments and rehabilitative services. It instead describes an orientation, an *approach* that can be adopted by any model, or any individual, today.

Roadblocks to Procovery

I remember asking around frantically about shock therapy and hypnosis, and anything under the sun short of lobotomies and suicide—always short of suicide—to relieve this unbelievable pressure, which I report now, not in the interest of laying on the agony, but simply to demonstrate how dark it can get just before total dawn, and how hard the last minutes of labor can seem when you're delivering a devil. —Wilfrid Sheed

It would be hellish enough if the only roadblock to procovery were the experience of illness and the limited resources available to most individuals and systems for treatment. Therefore, we must look closely at the unnecessary roadblocks that result from our misperceptions and misunderstanding of what is possible for individuals diagnosed with psychiatric illnesses.

Consumers and professionals alike often measure success against an ultimate goal of recovery, defined by Taber's Medical Dictionary[5] as the process of "regaining a former state of health." But recovery in this sense is often not an option, any more than one can undo a car wreck or the death of a loved one.

Pending this unavailable "recovery," treating professionals often have an extremely limited vision of what is possible for individuals with severe mental illness, and therefore offer a limited vision of the future—at best one of maintenance, one of surviving.

Low expectations lead to health care and support systems operating in such a way as to treat individuals as passive recipients rather than active participants. Consumers are often overlooked as a valuable resource in their own care and have little impact on their own treatment choices, resulting in decreased self-efficacy and increased non-compliance.

This situation is exacerbated by economic disincentives for individuals to rebuild their lives. For example, a distinct show of capability and increase in health could result in a loss of benefits such as Supplemental Security Income or Medicaid coverage and a discontinuation of the very service that may have substantially contributed to an individual's success.[4]

Stigma and prejudice further toughen the path of healing, creating an additional barrier against which overburdened and often underfunded mental health systems struggle to provide services.

Individuals diagnosed with psychiatric disabilities, and the people aiding them, may justifiably see a crisis not only in the disorder itself but also in society and the healing systems available to them.

Keep in mind, however, that the Chinese symbol for crisis connotes danger *and* opportunity.

In the middle of difficulty lies opportunity.
—Albert Einstein

What can each of us do despite the system of which, in fact, each one of us is a part? We can do more with less by doing differently.

Setting Favorable Conditions for Procovery

I am not interested in the past. I am interested in the future, for that is where I expect to spend the rest of my life. —Charles F. Kettering

Like gardening, procovery can best be initiated by setting up favorable conditions, planting more seeds than you expect to sprout, and nurturing the ones that do.

Favorable conditions are those that singly or together can significantly ease the path to healing. Like procovery itself, the conditions that are most favorable will differ among individuals. Here are eight conditions that I have seen to be important:

Believe that procovery is possible, that an individual diagnosed with chronic mental illness can overcome illness, integrating it into a productive and fulfilling life.

Recognize the power of the individual. As William Anthony, Ph.D., has said, "recovery can be facilitated by any one person."[7] Because procovery can be initiated or contributed to by any individual, at any time, procovery is most easily reached in a climate that fosters individual initiative—whether that of consumer, family, or staff.

Focus forward, not backward. Much can be accomplished when we let go of who we were and get to know who we are now and who we can become. Instead of trying to figure out, "Why did this happen to me?" "What could I have done to prevent it?" "What did I do to deserve it?" it is often more productive to ask, "What can I do about it?" and to move forward.

In the final analysis, the question of why bad things happen to good people translates itself into some very different questions, no longer asking why something happened, but asking how we will respond, what we intend to do now that it has happened.
—Harold S. Kushner

Focus on life rather than illness, and strengths rather than weaknesses, identifying and building on what is available. It has been said that teaching to draw is teaching to see; teaching procovery is teaching to recognize what *is* available in life.

Recognize that big problems don't necessarily need big solutions. It would be nice if there were one answer to feeling better, one exercise to do or one pill to take. But procovery is generally reached by an accumulation of helpful things. Small changes can have big impact.

I am done with great things and big plans, great institutions and big success. I am for those tiny, invisible loving human forces that work from individual to individual, creeping through the crannies of the world like so many rootlets, or like the capillary oozing of water, yet which, if given time, will rend the hardest monuments of human pride. —William James[vii]

Just start anywhere. There are as many paths to healing as there are paths to illness. The process of procovery begins by moving forward in any area, in any increment. Often our lives are so fragmented, just the thought of repair seems overwhelming. "Where do we start?" we wonder. Whether it's No. 1 or No. 5 or No. 30 on the task list, whether it's getting a goldfish or getting a job, just start anywhere.

Streams pour into creeks, creeks into rivers, and suddenly you have a Mississippi. —Carol Flinders, Ph.D.

Accept backsliding. The process of procovery is often two steps forward and one backward—or sometimes one step forward and two back. If we don't expect someone to make a perfect soufflé the first time, or win a marathon, or play a song on the piano, how can we expect an individual to procover from serious mental illness without setbacks or relapses? Backsliding is to be expected in any really difficult matter; it can be an indication of the difficulty of the task. Society applauds a persistent person who succeeds after repeated failure "against all odds," but beats the heck out of people while they are "failing."

The real challenge of rehabilitation programs is to create fail-proof program models. A program is fail-proof when participants are always able to come back, pick up where they left off, and try again.
—Patricia Deegan, Ph.D.

Keep hope alive. Positive emotions create positive reactions in the body, and negative emotions create negative reactions. While the biology of this is in dispute, the fact of it is not: hope is an enormous factor in healing. There is always reason to hope, and it is a central factor in successful procovery[9]—both as a broadly underlying condition and as an active strategy.

Clearly, hope is a life force in and of itself. A little hope —a remote chance for survival or a small improvement in one's condition—can give the strength to carry on.
—Ernest H. Rosenbaum, M.D. and Isadora R. Rosenbaum, M.A.[10]

Being able to effect your procovery doesn't mean you caused your illness. It doesn't mean that you were never mentally ill in the first place. It doesn't necessarily mean you're symptom free.

While procovery may result in the elimination of illness, this is not the focus. The focus of procovery is instead on the broader and more critical process of healing, of building life. That is, to master symptoms without necessarily eliminating them, and overcome illness without necessarily curing it.

Procovery Strategies

What we have to learn to do, we learn by doing.—Aristotle

So what specifically can individuals do to bring about procovery? A chapter of this book is devoted to each of the procovery strategies listed and then briefly discussed below:

Detoxifying the diagnosis. Use diagnosis only to the extent helpful. Individuals are not defined by their diagnoses. A diagnosis can be helpful, for example, to provide a starting point for treatments, can help put individuals in touch with each other for support, and can provide a label for further research. But at a certain point, a diagnosis becomes tremendously self-limiting.

Practical partnering in health care. Bernie Siegel, M.D., notes that "the most important kind of assertiveness a patient can demonstrate is in the formation of a participatory relationship with the doctor. Most patients don't talk to their doctors or ask a lot of questions for fear of angering this person who is going to 'make' them well." In mental health care, *compliance* and *choice* are often mirror images, and active partnering steps by professionals, consumers, and family members, within current systems, can radically improve the procovery process.

Medication management. Medication management is a two-way street. Although the physician has the power to "order" or write a prescription, the consumer (other than in the case of forced medication) has the ultimate power to take it or not. Yet in large part, consumers are left out of medication planning—choices, dosage, and timing—and frequently have their reported side effects invalidated or downplayed. Developing a collaborative medication management approach can increase compliance and greatly support the path to procovery.[11]

Uncovering hope. The intangibility of hope is in its measurement and not its effect. Hope can be found in what a person *can* do and what *is* available. Growing hope involves having faith in what is possible; recognizing and building on seeds of hope when they appear; and—most critically—not extinguishing it.

Creating change. Sometimes in the face of illness our dreams blow up in our face. It is important to

dream a new dream, and once you've done this to pick
some aspect of it and begin working toward it in any
increment.

Dissolving stigma. There is a great deal of talk
about stigma, meaning negative judgments and discrimination by others. But the most powerful and
destructive stigma of all is inner stigma. People diagnosed with mental illness often come to see themselves as damaged merchandise, not as strong, or
deserving, or likely to succeed as others. Individuals
can significantly move toward procovery by addressing
inner stigma *first*. It is often easier to have an impact
on yourself than on others, and helping yourself
strengthens you to impact others.

Using feelings as fuel. The anger, guilt, frustration,
and other feelings experienced along the path to procovery are too often seen as *symptoms*, rather than
consequences of illness and/or the procovery process.
Taking a procovery-oriented approach of moving forward through ordinary, individual actions, much can
be done not only to *cope* with feelings but also to use
feelings as *fuel* for procovery.

Gathering support. Procovery may or may not
involve the mental health system, but it is generally
not done alone. Finding ways to effectively invite and
accept support, as well as match the support to the
supporter, can make an enormous difference. William
Anthony, Ph.D., writes, "A common denominator of

recovery is the presence of people who believe in and stand by the person in need of recovery."[12]

Sticking with procovery when the going gets rough. Sometimes in the midst of crisis, all procovery efforts are abandoned or forgotten. But procovery efforts *during* crisis can greatly determine whether this particular crisis will be just part of the procovery process, a detour on the way to procovery, a turning point toward procovery, or a loss of will in getting there at all.

Self-care actions to take and choices to make. Illness can loom so deadening, so debilitating, so destructive that we assume it requires something strong, powerful, and exceptional to beat it. Self-care may seem too "anecdotal," too incidental to have an impact. But in fact self-care makes use of the most powerful medicine of all—the active participation of the individual.

Living intentionally through work and activities. Most simply stated, what we do all day matters. Although diagnosis may be specific, healing is holistic —involving medical, psychological, legal, family, spiritual, and financial components, many of which are impacted by one's approach to work and activities. Choices about work and activities can be made reactively or intentionally, and as a result, can increase the barriers or smooth the path to procovery.

Retaining procovery: the benefit of the bargain.
When taking a 10-day regimen of antibiotics, it is easier to remember to take them the first few days, while
the sickness is acute, than after the symptoms have
disappeared. Despite all the effort put into procovery,
it can be easy, once feeling better, to take improvement for granted and to downplay or simply forget the
importance of all the actions that made it possible.
Fortunately, the meaning and insight that results
from the process of procovery can provide individuals
their unique road map to retaining it.

Nurturing Procovery

There is no medicine like hope
No incentive so great
And no tonic so powerful
As the expectation
Of something better tomorrow.
　　—Orison Swett Marden[13]

If you want to work and send out one resume, you will
hope that one resume lands you a job. If you send out 50
resumes, you not only increase the odds but your faith in
the possibility of a positive outcome. This "upward spiral"
applies to procovery: If you take a procovery-oriented step,
no matter how small, you not only create a new possibility
of a positive outcome but—because that new possibility
exists—you build hope. And this hope, in turn, tends to
spur more positive action.

This is not to say that procovery is easy; it can be the greatest challenge of a life. As Fyodor Dostoyevsky wrote, "A new philosophy, a way of life is not given for nothing. It has to be paid dearly for, and only acquired with much patience and effort."

The difficulty of procovery is all the more reason to celebrate successes along the way, and to recognize that what might appear to be backsliding or "failure" can instead be an integral part of the process (and may in hindsight be seen as critical to having moved forward).

The voyage of the best ship is a zigzag line of a hundred tacks. See the line from a sufficient distance, and it straightens itself to the average tendency.
—Ralph Waldo Emerson

In fact, procovery is often understood best in hindsight. Just as you can drive from Miami to Los Angeles and not see a sign that you are on the way to California for more than 1,500 miles, the signs of procovery aren't always early or obvious.

The more we learn to seek out procovery the more obvious it becomes, the more subtle are the signposts that we can read, and the more available it begins to strike us. I am reminded of an anecdote by Kermit Long:

Two men were walking along a crowded sidewalk in a downtown business area. Suddenly one exclaimed:

"listen to the lovely sound of that cricket." But the other could not hear. He asked his companion how he could detect the sound of a cricket amid the din of people and traffic. The first man, who was a zoologist, had trained himself to listen to the voices of nature. But he didn't explain. He simply took a coin out of his pocket and dropped it on the sidewalk, whereupon a dozen people began to look about them. "We hear," he said, "what we listen for."

---

1. Anthony, W.A. (1993). "Recovery From Mental Illness: The Guiding Vision of the Mental Health Service System in the 1990s," *Psychosocial Rehabilitation Journal*, 16, p. 11-23.

2. I cannot recommend highly enough Erich Fromm's writings. By training a psychoanalyst, Fromm (who was born in Germany in 1900 and emigrated to the United States in 1934) was renowned as a teacher and a biblical scholar. His many excellent books include: *To Have or to Be?, The Sane Society, For the Love of Life,* and *The Art of Loving.* To echo a sentence from the jacket copy of *For the Love of Life*: Anyone concerned with the art of living will find his thoughts provocative, his advice sage, and his guidance gentle, down to earth, and infused with hope.

3. Keogh, C.B., ed. (1975). *Readings for Mental Health*, Maryborough, Australia: GROW Publications, Ltd., p. 216 (U.S. contact: GROW National Centre, Champaign, Illinois, 217-352-6989).

4. Neugeboren, Jay (1995). "Meanwhile Back on the Ward . . . ," *Psychiatric Rehabilitation Journal*, 19(2), p. 75-81.

5. *Taber's Cyclopedic Medical Dictionary*, F.A. Davis Company, 1993, p. 1682. Dictionaries emphasize the concept of "returning to" or "regaining" health, originating (according to Webster's) from the Middle French recoverer and the Latin recuperare.

6. Anthony, W.A. and Jansen, M.A. (1984). "Predicting the vocational capacity of the chronically mentally ill: research and policy implications," *American Psychologist*, 39

(5), 537-544.

7. Anthony, W.A. (1993). "Recovery From Mental Illness: The Guiding Vision of the Mental Health Service System in the 1990s," *Psychosocial Rehabilitation Journal*, 16, p. 1123.

8. Cited in Markova, Dawna(1991). *The Art of the Possible*, Conari Press, p. 222.

9. Blanch, A., Fisher, D., Tucker, W., Walsh, D. and Chassman, J. (1995). "Consumer-Practitioners and Psychiatrists Share Insights About Recovery and Coping," *Disability Studies Quarterly*, 13(2), 17-20.

10. Rosenbaum, Ernest H., M.D. and Rosenbaum, Isadora R., M.A. with Mandel, Mark, Cable, Greg, Anderson, Tina, and Gordon, Gail (1999). *Inner Fire: Your Will to Live, Stories of Courage, Hope and Determination*, Austin Texas: Plexus, p. 176.

11. "Perhaps the major problem compromising the potential effectiveness of acute phase pharmacotherapy is attrition from treatment before receipt of an adequate trial." Thase, M. and Kupfer, D. (1996). "Recent Developments in the Pharmacotherapy of Mood Disorders," *Journal of Consulting and Clinical Psychology*, 1996: 64(4): 646-659.

12. Anthony, W.A. (1993). "Recovery From Mental Illness: The Guiding Vision of the Mental Health Service System in the 1990s," *Psychosocial Rehabilitation Journal*, 16, p. 11-23.

13. Cited in Rosenbaum, Ernest H., M.D., and Rosenbaum, Isadora R., M.A. with Mandel, Mark, Cable, Greg, Anderson, Tina, and Gordon, Gail (1999). *Inner Fire: Your Will to Live, Stories of Courage, Hope and Determination*, Austin Texas: Plexus, p. 176.

Detoxifying the Diagnosis

Doctors make a diagnosis in fifteen minutes that it takes years to correct. —Russell D. Pierce, J.D.

The manner of giving and receiving a "chronically ill" diagnosis can have profound impact on the course of healing.

Much time, agony, and money can be saved by changing the message of diagnosis from a prescription of doom that initiates a cycle of despair to a delivery of information and hope that initiates a cycle of healing.

Just as many adults alive during the early 1960's vividly remember the day President John Kennedy was shot, many individuals experiencing chronic illness vividly remember the day they received a "chronic" diagnosis. And unfortunately that memory is often one of having their hopes and dreams shot down, of a day the lights went out or permanently dimmed.

"I want to offer them hope," a psychiatrist once told me, "but you know it's tough. These people have terrible problems I just can't fix. And for the life of me I can't come up with any reason for them to feel hopeful."

Yet if medications were prescribed with all of the pity and

focus on worst-case scenarios that accompanies the average chronic mental illness diagnosis, few individuals would ever take them.

The time of diagnosis is one of enormous opportunity, of enormous healing leverage. Hans Selye, M.D., notes, "It is well established that the mere fact of knowing what hurts you has an inherent cumulative value."[1]

This leverage is maximized by delivering *information in a hopeful manner*. Information should be clear as to the name of the diagnosis and treatment alternatives. Delivering this information in a hopeful manner includes communicating that, to the extent a particular illness is viewed as not curable, overcoming it, i.e., procovery, is possible.

It is essential to use a diagnosis *only to the extent helpful*. A diagnosis can provide a starting point for treatments, it can help put individuals in touch with each other for the purpose of support, and it can provide a box from which to do further research.

But it is essential to remember what a diagnosis is *not*. At a time when symptoms of illness tend to invade all aspects of life, it is critical not to allow illness to define who we are. Thinking of oneself as a diabetic, a schizophrenic, or any other diagnosis, has lasting echoes and repercussions on the path to procovery and the recognition that illness can be overcome, despite the limitations of symptoms and systems.

Therein lies an essential challenge for consumers, family, and staff—the challenge to give and receive a diagnosis in a manner that initiates a path to procovery, and begins the process of finding what is still available, rather than what isn't.

Procovery Notes for Consumers

❖ **Request written information** regarding a diagnosis. Receiving a diagnosis can be numbing. Having something to refer to later, when you're ready to absorb the next level of information, can be highly useful. See the second Procovery Note for Staff, below, for examples of the types of information that might be useful. Extensive information is also available via the web.

❖ **Get in touch with a procovered individual who shares the same diagnosis**. It can be a lifeline to get in touch with a procovered individual who has been there.

❖ **Recognize that statistics are not facts**. A diagnostic label is often accompanied by statistics purporting to predict treatment success, recovery rate, etc. Statistics frequently can predict how 1 one million people will vote in an election, but they can't predict how *you* will vote. Similarly, statistics can describe the effects of treatments on broad populations, but no statistics can determine how *you* will heal.

❖ **Sometimes the symptoms that lead to a diagnosis of serious mental illness can have at their root post-traumatic stress issues** such as with war veterans and victims of sexual and domestic abuse, and can be significantly impacted by alcohol and/or drug difficulties. In order to ensure that you are getting at the cause rather than the symptoms, consider opening a discussion of such traumatic experiences and drug or alcohol use with a trusted treating professional.

The problems of alcoholism and drug addiction have strong links to depression. The search for highs may often begin as a flight from lows.
—Nathan S. Kline, M.D.

❖ **So much important information gets passed at the time of diagnosis** that it might be helpful to bring a support person to your appointments to ask questions, gather information, and clarify answers.

❖ **If you have the option under your health plan or have the funds to do so, seek a second, unaffiliated opinion on both** the diagnosis and the suggested treatment approach.

Procovery Notes for Family Members

❖ **Recognize that much of the information related in the daze of diagnosis might be lost**. If you're at the appointment, taking notes can be helpful. If possible, try to confirm the accuracy before you leave, as medicalese can be confusing. This will give you an opportunity to make sure something has not been misunderstood.

❖ **Try to see that another appointment is set up soon to discuss treatment alternatives**. In the concern and confusion that might immediately follow a diagnosis of chronic mental illness, it can be helpful to know that you will speak to your treating professional soon, and have the ability to express concerns and ask questions. If you have a toothache, and you have a dentist appointment soon, you're not as worried and the pain tends to be less bothersome. Similarly, a follow-up visit scheduled soon after a diagnosis can reduce the natural fear, uncertainty, and anxiety experienced.

❖ **If it is possible, seek a second, unaffiliated opinion on both** the diagnosis and suggested treatment approach.

❖ **Help with research**. An incredible array of information is directly available to you, including through local support and advocacy groups; public, hospital, and college libraries; and on the Internet. Reference librarians will generally guide you through the library mazes, and posting a question on an on-line message board will likely get you directions on where to start on the Web.

⬥ **Avoid referring to anyone as their diagnosis.** Individuals are not "schizophrenics" or "manic-depressives" or any other illness. Although in our word-sensitive society, there is no agreement on the best words to use, consider "my daughter has been diagnosed with schizophrenia"—or *any* alternative that doesn't sum up an individual as an illness.

⬥ **Remind your loved one that a diagnosis doesn't impact your love or respect,** or your expectations for a meaningful life for them or for you. For many consumers, the diagnosis can feel like the beginning of the end. Your (frequent) affirmation that any diagnosis is just one little piece of their makeup, that their identity and your love for them has not been lost, can go a long way toward your loved one's acceptance of a diagnosis—and beginning a cycle of healing.

Procovery Notes for Staff

❖ **Deliver a diagnosis with a hopeful attitude** toward the experience of mental illness.

He could tell from my handshake that he didn't have to ask about my present condition, but he was eager to hear what was behind the recovery. It all began, I said, when I decided that some experts don't really know enough to make a pronouncement of doom on a human being. And I said I hoped they would be careful about what they said to others; they might be believed. And that could be the beginning of the end.
—Norman Cousins

❖ **Offer written information regarding the diagnosis.** Providing something to refer to later, when the next level of information is ready to be absorbed, is excellent practice. It is cost- and care-effective. Included with this information should be:

• General information regarding the diagnosis;

• Any information about treatment options;

• An emergency number, such as a hospital, a clinic, or a crisis hotline (chronic diagnoses can be terrifying later at home, when "it sinks in");

• Support group contacts;

• Any recommended reading.

◈ **Privately gather information as to past trauma and abuse**. As Timothy McCall, M.D., notes, childhood sexual abuse appears to be much more common than previously believed, may have major repercussions impacting diagnoses, and is generally undisclosed to a doctor.[2]

If a doctor can sensitively broach the subject of sexual abuse, important clues to current behavior and health problems can be obtained. If the patient does reveal a history of abuse, then interventions that go to the source of the problem, like therapy, may in the long run be much more effective than isolated efforts to suppress each symptom or modify each unhealthy behavior.
—Timothy McCall, M.D.[3]

◈ **Consider drug and alcohol use**. As Timothy McCall further notes, "Doctors should routinely incorporate questions about drug and alcohol use into the interview, even with people who show no signs of having a problem."

◈ **Support second opinions**. Don't discourage a second, unaffiliated opinion on both the diagnosis and the suggested treatment approach. A second opinion can increase confidence and likelihood of compliance, and can establish a foundation of trust for a long-term relationship.

Some patients, though conscious that their condition is perilous, recover their health simply through their contentment with the goodness of the physician.
—Hippocrates

❖ **If possible, put a consumer in touch with another consumer** who has procovered, or is in the process of doing so—preferably with their particular diagnosis.

My first afternoon, when I was admitted to the hospital, it was 4 o'clock in the afternoon. I was sitting on the edge of my bed. A man came through the door and sat next to me and said, "I'm your doctor; I'm here to help you." And what happened then is he got up and walked out the door, and the door closed. What should have happened at that point in time is that the door should have opened, and a person should have come in and sat down on the bed next to me and said, "Larry, I've had this illness. I am a consumer. There is life on the other side of this. And it can be quality life on the other side of this.

—Larry Schomer (on staff at Winnebago Mental Health Institute, and one of his responsibilities is to do just this)

---

1. Selye, Hans, M.D. (1956, 1976). *The Stress of Life*, New York, McGraw-Hill Book Co., 406.

2. McCall reports on a Mayo Clinic survey at a rural family practice clinic where more than 20 percent of the women patients revealed a history of childhood sexual abuse but fewer than 2 percent of them had ever told their physicians about the abuse. McCall, Timothy, M.D. (1995). *Examining Your Doctor*, New York, Birch Lane Press, 71.

3. *Id.*

Practical Partnering

"Basically, there's nothing wrong with you that what's right with you can't heal."

Force is all-conquering, but its victories are short lived.
—Abraham Lincoln

The choice of consumers and professionals to partner—or not to partner—has an incalculable impact on healing.

With the decreasing length of office visits, the increasing pharmacological focus of psychiatry, and the increasing importance of short-term measurable outcomes, if we want to be therapeutically and economically effective, partnering becomes more critical than ever.

Finding Mutual Benefit: Seeing Compliance and Choice as Mirror Images

Tell me, I'll forget. Show me, I may remember. But involve me and I'll understand. —Chinese Proverb

Significant research and professional attention is focused on the difficulties and cost of "non-compliance," that is, the failure of individuals to adhere to a prescribed treatment.[1] At the same time, consumers time and again express frustration over their lack of impact on their treatment plan, saying for example, "Doctors ignore my input because my qualifications are personal and not academic. In fact they argue with my observations about my own body, saying that I don't feel worse when I do, and denying my reactions to meds."[2]

The simple fact is that often consumers don't comply because they don't buy into the treatment plan, and often they don't buy into the treatment plan because they are not part of the decision-making process.

As James Gordon, M.D., writes,

> As long as doctors are trying to make or encourage patients to comply or adhere, both doctors and patients are in an impossible and debilitating bind. The assumption is that patients should comply because doctors have determined that their prescriptions are right for them and will be helpful to them. The implication is that if patients don't comply, there is something wrong either with them or with their

doctors or with both. Full compliance means everyone is doing his job. Anything less entails blame.

Demand for, or expectations of, compliance—no matter how qualified—are not only disrespectful and inappropriate but, as the literature shows, ineffective. They work poorly for chronic illness and indifferently in acute situations. Equally important, even when they do work—when the patient does do what she is told —they can help maintain her in an enduring state of passivity and dependence, which is itself likely to be unhealthy in the long run.

It would be far better and healthier for everyone concerned if we abandoned the very concepts of compliance and adherence and regarded the doctor-patient relationship as a full collaboration, a genuine healing partnership.[3]

It's Tough All Over: Understanding Each Other's Challenges

Always frame conflict as a clash of ideas, not persons.
—Robert Keegan

A poor understanding of each other's challenges can result in bad feelings and a missed opportunity to partner. For better or worse, all of the potential partners in the procovery process are human, subject to personal and organizational pressures, and to their own history of good and bad experiences.

Examples of some of the pressures and perspectives in chronic mental health care as of the writing of this book are offered below, not to establish what everyone in the procovery process is thinking but to stimulate potential partners to consider each other's perspectives in working toward a partnering strategy.

Health care organizations and administrators struggle with issues such as:

- How to meet the stiff demands of the marketplace, delivering good care to thousands, while doing it at the low price expected by those who pay the bills?

- How to prioritize limited funds for competing treatments: Restrict the formulary of available medications? Restrict, restructure, or eliminate therapy? Reduce coverage by more restrictive definitions of medical necessity?

- How to move toward meaningful and long-term outcomes for chronic conditions given the often short-term length of service contracts?

- Can they afford to include critical nonmedical services, such as vocational and housing support? Can they afford not to?

Psychiatrists are increasingly trying to rework their practice concepts into 10-minute med checks, cope with formularies that increasingly restrict their options, and learn to work within a managed care model.[4] Therapists are being squeezed by cost pressures, diminishing consumer confidentiality, and an increasingly narrow biological treatment focus.[5] Nurses, social workers, and staff across the board struggle with staffing and resource cuts, increased "productivity" responsibilities and demands, and intensifying use of protocols and guidelines that can seem inimical to individualized service.

Family members often feel out of the loop altogether, called with no hesitation in times of crisis but not included in treatment planning. Family members want to know more about a diagnosis and medications and other treatment options, and how to best support their loved ones —not just be called by emergency room personnel or a police officer at 2 a.m. because of a psychiatric crisis.

Consumers cope not only with the hell of illness but often with the seemingly equal hell of treatment. The confusion of often uncoordinated physical and mental health services. The reduction of therapy as an option, combined with the contraction of office visits. The expansion of pharmacological alternatives and the shrinking of health plan formularies of covered medications.[6] Many plans reduce costs by requiring one and sometimes two of the older medications fail before a newer one will be prescribed.

On top of all this, shifts in services, formularies and treating professionals buffet consumers, fueling fear and uncertainty. The medication finally stabilized on after a year and to which a consumer attributes his very sanity— sorry, it's not on the new plan. The professionals with whom a consumer has invested substantial time and trust to finally develop a working relationship—sorry, they are no longer on the "network."[7]

Many consumers and professionals are concerned about the impact of reduced privacy of their mental health care records. For example, more and more employers have information about their employees' health, and more and more of them use it in personnel decisions. The stigmatizing impact of a psychiatric diagnosis can be enormous. In addition, as a practical matter, consumers are increasingly being asked, in exchange for therapy, to accept the surrender of confidentiality.[8]

Changing the Chemical Mixture: How One Person Can Impact the Partnership

If everybody is thinking alike, then somebody isn't thinking.
—General George S. Patton

To paraphrase Carl Jung, relationships are like chemical mixtures; if you alter one chemical, the mixture not only will not but *cannot* remain the same.

In this same manner, individuals have significant and often unexpected, power to impact a healing partnership through their own actions. And since we obviously have more control over ourselves than we do over others, it makes sense to consider what those actions might be.

Perhaps the place to illustrate the opportunity and availability of approaches to partner is at the toughest point in any healing partnership—where there are differences of opinion.

In the context of procovery, differences should be embraced as natural and, more important, as therapeutically positive. Differences, if discussed, can be an opportunity to establish a treatment plan that will stick.

From a professional perspective, open airing of and working through differences can cement trust, increase the likelihood of treatment compliance, and reduce the likelihood of grievance or malpractice claims.[9] Writes Timothy McCall, M.D., "For the most part, people sue doctors they don't like. If a patient finds a doctor arrogant, withdrawn, or unconcerned and *then* something goes wrong, the result may be a lawsuit. But if the relationship is good, patients seldom sue."[10] Studies on the motives of malpractice plaintiffs have shown that more than 80 percent felt embittered by the doctor's response to their complaints and questions. And more than half of the malpractice suits are said to be the result of poor physician-patient communication.[11]

From a consumer perspective, airing differences is often the only way to change treatment, such as a medication dosage or a rehabilitation plan, which may be essential to moving forward. At the same time, airing differences may create a risk of retribution.

So what strategies are available to air and work through differences in a productive manner, and build a healing partnership?

Build a track record worthy of trust. Then when a difference arises, it is likely to be either easier to resolve or easier to leave unresolved (agreeing to disagree). Building a track record means, for example, arriving at appointments prepared and on time, being honest about treatment information and decisions, following through on whatever you've agreed to do, etc.

See if you can mutually restate and agree on treatment goals. It's easier to build agreement from a common set of goals. Many times mutually clarifying goals clears up miscommunication and opens up new ways to proceed.

Offer some area of flexibility. Obviously, finding a win-win opportunity is ideal, but *both* parties offering flexibility will show the good faith often necessary to turn a conflict into a collaboration. Perhaps agreeing to give a treament a shot for a specific period of time, or agreeing to consider a second opinion, etc.

Separate the decision from the heat of emotion. Some decisions, especially when discussion becomes volatile, are better not resolved immediately. A "can I get back to you" stance, to allow for cooling off, with a definite (and not lengthy) time frame agreed upon for decision, can be a pragmatic way to provide a period to find additional alternatives and improve decision-making from both sides.

Pick your battles. Staff might like consumers to adhere in all ways, to show motivation, etc. Consumers might like staff to include them in all treatment planning, to be open to, knowledgeable and supportive of alternatives, etc. Working together doesn't mean agreeing on everything, but being able to work through and find common ground in areas that matter most to each.

S. Haiman, M.D., writes, "In mental health, the practitioner-patient relationship has undergone one tremendous paradigm shift and is now undergoing another. First the shift from hospital-based to community-based practice, and now emphasis on client autonomy, self-direction and personal power, where the patient is viewed as a competent agent of change and practitioners are asked to see the patient less as a patient or client and more as a colleague. We have only scratched the surface of what it means to engage in collaborative efforts with individual clients."

This collaborative challenge is what Erich Fromm broadly describes as the challenge to *exercise rational authority*, as opposed to irrational authority: "Irrational authority is based on power and serves to exploit the person subjected to it; by creating dependence, it tends to institutionalize itself. Rational authority is based on competence and helps the person who leans on it to grow; it tends to dissolve itself as it achieves its goal."[12]

If we ignore partnering opportunities, we do so at our own peril. Like the boss who refuses to delegate, the professionals, consumers, and family members who fail to adopt partnering approaches miss an enormous opportunity to maximize the available resources, on all sides. They also miss an enormous opportunity for a classic case of win-win-win—reduced costs, increased compliance, and, most important, improved healing.

Procovery Notes for Consumers

❖ **Educate yourself**. Whether it is information regarding a particular diagnosis, available treatments, medications, or alternatives, do not assume your doctor knows everything. With the breakneck pace of information creation and change, this is impossible. In addition, your doctor is likely to be faced with major time, resource, and organizational constraints. The best doctor, rather than knowing everything, admits what he doesn't know and finds—or suggests where you can likely find—the answer. Work with your doctor, learning from and educating him. Information, like the telephone, can and should go both ways. See the Procovery Note for Family Members in the chapter "Detoxifying the Diagnosis" that discusses research possibilities.

❖ **Develop a destination**. Often symptom management is the primary if not sole focus of doctor visits. Symptom management is critical, but the path to procovery entails more. And yet how can there be more without clear communication? Imagine if you were trying to get subway directions in New York City, but

you could only say where you *didn't* want to go—you'd
be in for a long trip!

*It's just as difficult to reach a destination you don't
have, as it is to come back from a place you've never
been.* —Zig Ziglar

Unfortunately, this is how some health care is han-
dled. It is easy to assume more commonality than
exists. To avoid competing agendas (or non-agendas),
it is important to develop, preferably with your doctor,
a destination, both short- and long-term.

Some possible destinations are:

- stabilizing on a medication

- improving mood

- improving sleep

- relieving side effects

- joining or starting a support group

Remind your doctor of your objectives at the beginning of each visit. You might request that a reminder
of these objectives be kept in your file, and that you
both refer to these objectives as a refresher at the
beginning of each appointment.

❖ **Organize for appointments**. In an ideal world, we would have all the time we needed with treating professionals. In reality, we don't. It is important to use the small amount of time (and getting smaller) that we do have to our best advantage. If possible, confirm in advance how much time you will have; otherwise, ask as soon as your visit begins. If there is information you know the doctor will want (e.g., name and dosage of any other medications you are taking, prescription or over-the-counter) or questions he will ask (e.g., how your medications are working, side effects, sleeping, eating, mood), be prepared.

But don't just organize for what your doctor will want, organize for what you want. If you have a specific goal for a visit, such as a new symptom or a concern regarding medication, bring it up immediately—don't wait until the end. Maximize every minute you have with your doctor.

❖ **Ask specific, direct questions**. Reynolds Price, author of "A Whole New Life," tells a story of continual visits to doctors' offices for treatment of extensive cancer and its by-product, tremendous physical pain. He says that he could only assume these good, caring doctors, nurses, orderlies, and physical therapists would have alleviated the pain if possible. It was only after two years of continuing agony that a doctor mentioned for the first time the possibility of biofeedback training—*offered in the same building*—through which he was able to achieve incredible reduction in the pain.[13] Examples of specific questions are:

- Do you have anything I can take with me to read about this diagnosis?

- What interactions are there between my medications and over-the-counter drugs and/or alcohol?

- What is the optimum time to determine whether this new medication is working (in other words, how long do I take it before I can try something else)?

- Is there a time period after I go off this medication before I can begin another one?

- What options are there in addition to or other than medication?

- Or at times the best question of all to ask a doctor —What do you think I should be asking right now?

- Above all, BE DIRECT.

❖ **Do not assume you have no choice in your doctor or other treating professional**. It is worth recognizing that many times psychiatric relationships (like all relationships) get into a tough area, and it is important to work this through and not to give up on the relationship.

If, however, you feel you are in a dead-end relationship, do not assume you need to remain there. Many times options exist but aren't explored. It is important to explore options and ask questions in such a way that it won't fuel the fire; something like, "I'm thinking maybe we're not on the same wavelength. I was wondering if you feel the same."

❖ **Recognize that statistics are not facts.** See the Procovery Note for Consumers in the chapter "Uncovering Hope" that discusses the use and misuse of statistics.

❖ **Complete an advance directive.** Many states have laws that give you the right to make health care decisions in advance, through instructions called "advance directives." An advance directive can be used to name a health care agent—that is, someone to make health care decisions for you—in the event you are ever judged incompetent. An advance directive can also be used to make clear your treatment preferences, especially about procedures that might be used to sustain your life.

According to the Bazelon Center for Mental Health Law, "While advance directives for health care have been around a long time, their use for psychiatric care is a very new area of law. We do not yet know how courts will deal with them, especially when safety issues arise. State laws vary and it is possible that part or all of this document will not be effective in your state. However, many mental health consumers who are now using these documents find that an advance directive increases the likelihood that doctors, hospitals, and judges honor their choices." Your local state protection and advocacy group (to find yours, contact the National Association of Protection and Advocacy Systems at 202-408-9514 or www. protectionandadvocacy.com) should be able to help you find your local group.

Possibly the most important aspect of an advance directive is your choice of advocate(s). Don't necessarily choose the person you love the most; choose the person who best understands and will be the best advocate for *your* goals and needs.

❖ **Address boundaries**. It can be uncomfortable to be called by your first name while your doctor expects to be "Dr. Smith." Or to week after week spill your gut, sharing your innermost thoughts to your therapist, and one afternoon at the end of a session to ask casually, "Do you have children?" to have your therapist bristle, saying, "I never discuss my personal life with my patients." Or to call your doctor in the middle of the night in a crisis, only to be met with anger.

Boundaries exist in any therapeutic relationship. It is important to address these boundaries early on.

❖ **Communicate**. Maybe you've been referred by your psychiatrist to an internist for a test. That right there can prove challenging. For as one consumer said,

"Internists dismiss my concerns when they learn I have a psychiatric diagnosis—they think I'm imagining the problem and say they can't do anything for me." Maddeningly enough, a psychiatric diagnosis can stand in the way of receiving quality health care in other areas. If it would be helpful, ask your psychiatrist to assist you in developing a clear description of why he or she has referred you and of any symptoms you might have. This can make a significant difference in how seriously the internist takes your input and the ease with which he or she is able to make a diagnosis.

You have severe abdominal pains again in the middle of the night. The last time the Emergency Room doctor said to come over right away when you get the pains, to better diagnose them. So you go. A different ER doctor is there. He asks you the preliminary questions. Then he comes to, 'Are you taking any medications?' After you name the psychotropic drugs you're on, his face changes to one of skepticism. Suddenly he doesn't believe the pains are real. He finds nothing in his examination. And he says he does not have any notes from any other ER doctor (though your last visit was only a week ago). He doesn't believe you. You're malingering, or hypochondriacal, or psychotic, or worse. You know the truth. But the truth can't be believed: you're only a CMI. —Betty Blaska, M.A.[14]

❖ **Communicate more**. Consumers often have more than one treating professional—psychiatrists, nurses, social workers, internists, therapists, primary care doctors. This can pose unique challenges. As consumers note, "You rarely meet with both your psychiatrist and therapist—charts get lost between the two and they don't communicate." "The records don't follow the patient— sometimes they get lost." "My doctor doesn't keep up with the therapist, and my therapist says, 'Ask the doctor.'" This obviously shouldn't be your problem, but unfortunately it can be.

There are times when you might greatly benefit from three-way communication with you and your treating professionals together. For example, you might agree with your primary care doctor, internist, or therapist that during an upcoming, regularly scheduled appointment, you will talk together via speakerphone with your psychiatrist.

❖ **Communicate still more**. There is often little if any communication or continuity between inpatient and outpatient care. This can lead to costly, often dangerous mistakes. Immediately upon your admittance to the hospital, staff should be informed that you have an advance directive (if you do). They should also be advised if you have an outpatient doctor, and you or your advocate should request that your inpatient and outpatient doctors talk to each other as soon as possible.

Do not assume that this will happen—you (or anyone advocating on your behalf) will need to follow up to make sure it does.

◈ **Reach for prevention**. Preventing a crisis situation is obviously more desirable than dealing with one. And yet, when numbing feelings of depression or any other warning signs surface, the emotions themselves may make it difficult to take preventive steps. The reverse is also true; when someone is feeling on top of the world, he or she rarely gives any thought to preventing illness. Check out the chapter of this book, "Sticking With Procovery When the Going Gets Rough."

◈ **Know what to do in a crisis**. Crises are key trigger points both in treatment and in life. The delicate balance in which we live can be destroyed by not knowing what to do. See the Chapter of this book, "Sticking With Procovery When the Going Gets Rough."

◈ **Look outside the system**. The health system is inadequate to treat the nature and impact of serious health problems, as they mushroom to include physical, mental, financial, legal, family, social, and spiritual components. So although there is much available in the health system, trying to get 16 ounces of soda out of an eight-ounce can just isn't going to work. Once you have defined your destination and found what is available to you within the system, then also look outside the system. Maybe it is you taking the lead in forming a support group, or self-care, or alternative medicine. None of these may be the elusive "cure," and no one solution may exist, but along the way many small things can have a positive impact and ultimately snowball into procovery. Check out the chapter of this book, "Exercising Self-care: Actions to Take and Choices to Make."

Procovery Notes for Family Members

❖ **Offer to serve as a reminder for appointments**.

❖ **Offer to help organize ahead of time for appointments**, perhaps collecting some of the following information: any improvement noted, anything worse, any additional issues or concerns, any other professionals seen, and any treatments or medications they prescribed.

❖ **Offer to accompany to and/or take notes at appointments**.

❖ **Make efficient use of meeting/staff time**. Do not ask staff to do things outside of their area of responsibility. Don't ask them for information easily accessed elsewhere. Don't make unreasonable demands, clearly outside their authority, resources, or expertise.

◈ **It can be a tough balance to find the optimum level of involvement**. As one father noted, "I have felt squeezed out of the most important treatment decisions—but I have to live with the consequences of them." Offer to be involved in any and all aspects of treatment planning.

◈ **Set up some type of family communication system** —perhaps establishing a point person and phone tree—so family members communicate through each other rather than staff.

◈ **Be organized and direct**. Ask specific questions.

Procovery Notes for Staff

◈ **Mental health consumers must be welcomed as partners in their care**, in assuming a significant degree of control in the development of their treatment plan, and in determining the goals toward which they choose to work. Consumer choice must exist![15]

It's a lot easier to fight an illness when you don't have to fight the doctor as well. —Wilfrid Sheed[16]

◈ **Deliver a diagnosis, not a prescription of doom**. Epictetus said, "Men are disturbed not by things which happen, but by the opinions about the things." See the notes for staff in the chapter, "Detoxifying the Diagnosis."

◈ **Keep in mind, as William Flynn, M.D., notes, that often "In the beginning of the treatment relationship, you're just symbolic to the client,** not a real person; you might just represent the people they've had bad experiences with. So it's critical to stick in there with the person, let them rage if necessary. That's crucial time, at the beginning of the relationship, when you don't want to just chase them away."

◈ **Share written information** about diagnosis, treatment options, support groups, crisis hotlines, numbers to call outside of regular office hours. It can be hard to absorb all of the information given during a visit for both consumers and staff. Having something in writing to take home or put in the file can be helpful.

No prescription is more valuable than knowledge.
—C. Everett Koop, former U.S. Surgeon General

◈ **Offer choice to the fullest extent possible**. Offering two viable treatment options, and explaining why you believe one treatment option is superior, is better than *ordering* one specific treatment.

◈ **Make sure everyone is clear on "roles."** Consumers have said that there have been times they were angry at their physicians for six months for hurrying them through their therapy sessions, before they became aware they were not scheduled for therapy—or covered by insurance for therapy—only for a 10-minute med check.

◈ **Develop a common destination**, both short and long term, to avoid two different competing agendas (or non-agendas).

◈ **Focus less on gaining compliance than on building self-reliance**. Don't assume non-compliance is the reason for non-success. When a seed doesn't sprout, a gardener considers whether the conditions aren't right.

◈ **Develop a relapse prevention and crisis plan**. Preventing a crisis is usually more desirable than dealing with one. Crises are key trigger points both in treatment and in life. The delicate balance in which we live can be destroyed by not knowing what to do. Consider the use of advance directives to help with these plans. See the Procovery Note for Consumers above on advance directives, and the chapter of this book, "Sticking With Procovery When the Going Gets Rough."

◈ **Recognize that what works for one person doesn't necessarily work for another**, or even for the same person over a period of time.

◈ **Avoid the natural tendency to attribute everything to illness**.

◈ **Accept backsliding as a natural part of the procovery process**. Stories abound that when consumers backslide they are punished by the system or made to feel worse. This is unrealistic and counterproductive.

◈ **Speak to communicate**, not in medicalese or other jargon.

◈ **When partnering with individuals that have experienced trauma and/or abuse**, keep in mind that these individuals may have been been traumatized or abused for taking the very steps necessary to part-ner—being assertive, developing trust, sharing infor-mation, making decisions. You hold enormous power in your interactions with these individuals to build their self-efficacy and self-esteem and their ability to partner.

◈ **Instead of saying, "Here's what you need," and, "Here's what I'm going to do for you,"** try, "Tell me what you want," or, "Tell me what you need," or "I wonder if you might be willing to try something," or perhaps best of all, "Let's see what we might be able to do, together."

The best policy when you do not know, or even when you do know what to do, is to ask the person what she needs: 'What will help you?' —Betty Blaska, M.A.[15]

◈ **Give individuals the benefit of the doubt**. Gotthold Lessing said, "There are things which must cause you to lose your reason or you have none to lose."[18] Many times, an individual's actions, while perhaps seeming irrational, are in fact a sane reaction to an insane sit-uation.

◈ **Foster a JUST START ANYWHERE mode of consumer action**. Procovery does not have one starting point, or one destination. Whether it is No. 1, No. 5 or No. 30 on a task list, the goal is just to start moving forward, in any area, in any increment. There are as many paths to healing as there are paths to illness.

---

1. In fact, consumer "non-compliance" has acquired its own code (V15.81) in the *Diagnostic and Statistical Manual of Mental Disorders*.

2. *Health Action Network Letter*, 1996.

3. Gordon, James, M.D. (1996). *Manifesto for a New Medicine*, New York: Addison-Wesley Publishing Co., 86-87.

4. Jeremy Lazarus, Denver psychiatrist and consultant to the managed care committee of the American Psychiatric Association, says, "Instead of working just with the patient, now there's an 800-pound gorilla in the room." (*US News*, 1/19/98) Joseph Kwentus, psychiatrist at Tennessee Christian Medical Center, agrees with this concerned assessment: "You're not very much in control of what happens to the patient anymore." Nancy Menke, Tennessee Health Commissioner, counters, "We're not surprised that the psychiatrists have problems with the program. I'd just as soon nobody told me what to do either. That's just life." (*Wall Street Journal*, 1/14/98)

5. Managed care companies readily admit to denying coverage for "unfocused therapy for interpersonal growth and development." Some therapists bristle at the suggestion that their work is expendable, but others refocus consumers largely into "brief therapy" and group therapy techniques. At age 50, Peter Janney has been in practice for more than 20 years, and he is looking for a new career. He closed a practice in Cambridge, Mass., last year and now sees a handful of private patients in Brookline and Salem. He ekes out a living doing psychological evaluations for nursing homes, but is actively seeking to get out of the field. "As I cross the threshold at age 50, I didn't envision I'd be doing this," says Janney, a psychologist who was on the steering committee of the Consortium of Psychotherapy, an advocacy group. "It's been shattering. It's a major life crisis. Frankly, I don't understand why anybody is enrolling in graduate programs for psychology or social work these days." (*Boston Globe*, 10/16/98)

6. A 1998 National Alliance for the Mentally Ill report card surveying nine of the country's largest behavioral health managed-care companies (and flunking all of them). Among the findings were that some plans still prescribed Haldol—a decades-old drug with side effects including severe and irreversible tremors—for schizophrenia rather than newer, more expensive drugs like Clozipine and Risperdal. (*US News*, 1/19/98)

7. "I don't want managed care because I am afraid I would have to receive all my services from a limited selection of practitioners. I have taken care and time to build my own support system!"—quote from a 1996 Health Action Network survey of consumers in Wisconsin.

8. "The more specific you are, the more dirty laundry you give them, the more approvals you get," says Jennifer Katze, a Baltimore psychiatrist. "As a result, managed mental health care is slowly pushing the patient-therapist relationship toward conversation that begins to resemble that of a police officer and a suspect. Psychiatrists speak of "Miranda-izing" their new patients—warning them that whatever they say may end up in an information stream to which the patient may have no easy access and over which the patient may have no control." (*Washington Post*, 2/8/98)

9. James Gordon, M.D., writes about the "profoundly deforming effect that the fact and threat of malpractice suits exert on American medicine," and the "counterproductive, adversarial atmosphere [concern over malpractice] brings to medical practice." Gordon, James, M.D. (1996). *Manifesto for a New Medicine*, New York: Addison-Wesley Publishing Co., 267.

10. McCall, Timothy, M.D. (1995). *Examining Your Doctor*, New York, Birch Lane Press, 106. See also A. Russell Localio, *et. al.*(1991). "Relation between malpractice claims and adverse events due to negligence: Results of the Harvard Medical practice study," *New England Journal of Medicine*, July 25, 1991; 235(4) 245-50. This study of 31,000 hospital records in New York state found that one percent of these patients had legitimate claims for injury and compensation, but only two percent of those approximately 300 patients ever filed a claim.

11. Gordon, James, M.D. (1996). *Manifesto for a New Medicine*, New York: Addison-Wesley Publishing Co., 267.

12. As discussed in much of Fromm's writings. For example, see *The Sane Society* (1955), New York: Hold, Rinehart & Winston, 90-95.

13. Price, Reynolds (1982). *A Whole New Life: An Illness and a Healing*, New York: Penguin Books, 112, 154.

14. Blaska, Betty (1995). "What it's like to be treated like a CMI" (chronically mentally ill), *The Mental Health System: Consumer Survival Guide*, 39.

15. Crowley, Kathleen (1997). "Implementing the Concept of Recovery," *The Blue Ribbon Commission on Mental Health Final Report*, State of Wisconsin, April 1997, 15.

16. Sheed, Wilfred (1995). *In Love With Daylight: A Memoir of Recovery*, New York: Simon and Schuster, 21.

17. Blaska, Betty (1994). "Expanded Notes from Mendota Training Seclusion & Restraint," *Emerging Force*, July/Aug 1994.

18. Lessing, Gotthold Ephraim (1772). *Emilia Galotti.* Also quoted in Frankl, Victor (1959). *Man's Search for Meaning.* Washington Square Press, 38.

Managing Medications

Professionals, for their part, need to listen to consumers more attentively. However, I hold consumers more responsible for correcting these errors, because I believe we must take responsibility for our lives and our treatment.
—Betty Blaska, M.A.[1]

At the [government regulatory program] they have found they get much better compliance with guidelines rather than mandatory restrictions. There is a certain percent of the population who won't comply regardless and those who do comply regardless. You are left with those who will cooperate if asked and rebel if threatened. —Web posting

Increasingly, medication is the primary focus of treatment in mental health plans and systems.[2] With substantially heightened focus on and funding for medication research, there has been a vast increase in the number of medications available for treating mental illness. Some name advances in medication as the single most potent force in changing mental health care since the 1950s.[3]

But these medications can come at a cost. They often create their own havoc, with "side" effects that worsen the situation before improving it. They may act as a sedative or depressant. They may have severe, even deadly interactions with other medications, with food, with alcohol, with pregnancy, with extreme heat. It can take weeks or months to stabilize on a medication, during which the side effects can be even more pronounced. It may be the third or fourth medication that is most helpful, but each one has its own trial period, and many must be followed by a medication-free period to clear out the system. Many of the newer medications that have reported fewer side effects are significantly more expensive and often aren't covered under the insurance or health plan—or if they are in the formulary, there may be a prerequisite of prior unsuccessful trials with less expensive drugs.

William Styron, in *Darkness Visible*, described his own medication experience: "The pill made me edgy, disagreeably hyperactive, and when the dosage was increased after 10 days, it blocked my bladder for hours one night. Upon informing Dr. Gold of this problem, I was told that 10 more days must pass for the drug to clear my system before starting anew with a different pill. Ten days to someone stretched on such a torture rack [as clinical depression] is like ten centuries—and this does not begin to take into account the fact that when a new pill is inaugurated, several weeks must pass before it becomes effective, a development which is far from guaranteed in any case."[4]

The simple truth is that medication management is at times an extraordinarily sensitive balancing act. Jerry Dincin, Ph.D., notes, "Every person's reaction to medication is idiosyncratic as to the most effective medication or combination of medications and the correct dosage. And every person's reaction to secondary effects is different. This makes the administration of medication subject to trial and error, a kind of scientific art form."[5]

These difficulties are not a minor aspect of the treatment of chronic mental illness. In fact, difficulties with medication management comprise a major portion of consumer complaints. And health care staff view failures of consumers to take their medications as prescribed ("non-compliance") as one of the major problems facing mental health treatment.

As a result, there is enormous therapeutic and economic gain to be had by dramatically improving how medications are offered and received.

Don't Tell; Engage

Prescriptions are often handed out at the end of a visit with the assumption they will be taken—for why wouldn't they? Who in the midst of a fire wouldn't want to use the fire extinguisher handed to them?

Consumers frequently have a very different point of view. Imagine feeling worse than you ever felt it was humanly possible to feel, and someone offers you the possibility of relief—but it might take a couple of months and it may not work at all and you may feel even worse almost immediately.

In addition, although people might jump at medication for a serious infection or for life-threatening high blood pressure, the idea of taking a medication whose purpose is to alter your brain chemistry is inherently terrifying. And taking a "psychiatric" medication can feel embarrassing because of the stigma attached to mental illness in general.

Add to these concerns a mistrust that often arises between consumers and treating professionals because the doctor is the only one who can write a prescription, and consumers often feel intensely the burden of illness without power over their treatment.

And yet, although doctors clearly have the power to prescribe, the consumer has the ultimate power (other than with forced medication) to take or not to take the medication.

If the medication management goal of consumers and treating professionals is identical—to stabilize not only in the short term but also over the long term—medication compliance and choice must be seen as mirror images.

As noted in the chapter on "Practical Partnering," treating professionals can help individuals move toward procovery and increase compliance by offering information and choice, actively engaging them in their treatment process. A wide range of specific ideas are included in the Procovery Notes for this chapter, but the broad strategy is to recognize that successful medication management is a mutual process of finding what works best for a specific individual, which gives the individual both a responsibility and an opportunity. Incremental choices, such as timing and dosage, may be therapeutically empowering, even where there can be no effective choice in the medication itself (for example, due to formulary restrictions).

At the same time, individuals can develop more effective medication management strategies by building upon and communicating to staff, their knowledge and experience about their own bodies and about what works and doesn't; and by taking advantage of self-care steps to reduce the negative effects of medications. The Procovery Notes at the end of this chapter include a variety of medication management collaboration ideas.

How can a staff member draw a consumer into treatment planning if the consumer shows no interest? How can a consumer involve himself in treatment planning if staff shows no interest in him doing so?

Changing the Chemistry

Treat people as if they were what they ought to be, and you help them become what they are capable of becoming.
—Goethe

In the long run it takes two to tango, but remember that in the short term someone has to start the dance. Any individual—consumer, family member, or staff—can make a difference in managing medications toward procovery by taking a single step toward changing the chemistry of the medication management relationship.

Even if a doctor shows no interest in offering choice, a clear commitment by a consumer to stay with an agreed-upon treatment plan for a specific period of time—if certain changes in the plan take place—can sometimes help a doctor to see reason to compromise.

Even if a consumer shows no interest in treatment planning or medication choices, interest and assertiveness can be effectively encouraged. Betty Blaska, M.A., wrote, "I think it is important to remind both the public and professionals that many mistakes are made in prescribing drugs, that psychotropic drug side effects can be harrowing, and that mentally ill patients often become frustrated and quit taking their medications when mistakes are not corrected. In addition, I think consumers who take medications—and most of us will continue to take them—need frequent admonitions to become more assertive in our psychiatrist-patient relationships and to take the lead in voicing complaints, observations, and preferences."[6]

Like all procovery strategies, partnering in medication management is not just a strategy to increase the effectiveness of medications, but is a principal therapeutic activity in itself that can start the snowball to procovery.

Procovery Notes for Consumers

❖ **Learn about your options regarding medications**. Doctors, nurses, and pharmacists can often provide free written information for you to take home—ask for it. As you talk with staff and read the information, here are some questions to consider:

- How are you hoping the medication will help me? What is the medication's success rate in doing so for others?

- What other medications are most commonly prescribed for this diagnosis, and why are you recommending this one?

- Are there any long-term risks associated with this medication? Is it addictive? How would you weigh the benefits against the possible risks?

- Does the medication go by any other names? (If you are researching a medication, you might need to know these other names.)

- Does this medication work right away, or does it take some time to work?

- Am I likely to feel worse before I feel better? How long before I am likely to see improvement?

- What is the trial period for determining whether this medication is working?

- How will we judge whether the medication is working?

- What is the exit strategy if the medication isn't working (i.e., how long to taper off, how long before I can start a new one)?

- What are the common side effects of this medication?

- Are there any lab tests that need to be done (eg., heart test, blood test) before or while I am taking the medication? How often will progress need to be checked and who will check it?

❖ **Once you've chosen a medication**, here are some additional medication-specific questions to ask:

- Are there any particular interactions I should be aware of between this medication and certain foods? And alcohol?

- Are there any particular interactions I should be aware of between this medication and drugs, including over-the-counter? (Bring a list of the ones you're currently taking, and check your medicine cabinet for any others you may take on occasion.)

- Are there any things that could happen while I'm taking this medication that I should report immediately to my doctor? That I should wait and tell my doctor about at my next appointment?

- Is there anything I can do to prevent or minimize side effects?

- Should I do anything special when I take it, such as drink a glass of water, take it with food, or take it on an empty stomach?

- Do I need to keep the medication in a special place?

- What should I do if I forget to take a dose?

- If I get worse while taking this medication, should I take more?

- If I feel better on a particular day, can I skip a dose?

❖ **Establish a medication routine**. It can be difficult to remember whether you've taken a particular dose of medication. Keep your medication in one specific place, with a check-off list to keep track of whether you've taken it. Try to integrate the taking of medication into your usual routine of the day—e.g., getting up, going to bed, eating meals, brushing teeth. Sometimes it helps to pre-package tablets in individual envelopes labeled as to date and time of day for taking.

❖ **Establish reminder systems**. A digital watch with an alarm can be a useful reminder. Choosing a supporter (not an enforcer) can help until you've adjusted to the routine of taking medication. If you find that you just cannot remember to take the medication, discuss alternative dosing with your doctor.

- ❖ **If you get varying instructions regarding your medication** (from a pharmacist, additional doctor, nurse, family member, etc.) call your doctor or have your pharmacist call your doctor to confirm which is optimum.

- ❖ **Be sure other treating doctors** (and dentists) know what psychotropic medications you are taking or have recently taken.

- ❖ **Many psychotropic drugs are known to increase risk for developing heat stroke.**[7] During heat waves, try to stay in the shade or inside with air conditioning as much as possible. Drink lots of fluids (juice, water, and caffeine-free soda). Avoid alcoholic beverages, coffee, and soda with caffeine, as they will make you more dehydrated. Avoid strenuous exercise and, if you are miserably hot, a cool shower or cold cloth on your forehead may help.

- ❖ **Celebrate completion of a trial period of medication**. Even if the medication didn't work, celebrate the effort. Like scientific research, learning what doesn't work is often a critical step to finding what does.

- ❖ **Before discontinuing a possibly promising medication because of side effects**, consider whether altering the dosage or time of day might help. For example someone taking a medication at bedtime and experiencing extreme morning fatigue might move the evening dose earlier to dinner or late afternoon.

❖ **Sometimes after a period of stabilization, the medication might not seem to be working as well.** Try to determine whether this is so. It is important not to attribute every change to medication. Could it be that you are now working (something you could not have done pre-medication), or recently moved, or just received sad news, or are recovering from a flu?

Procovery Notes for Family Members

❖ **Offer to assist with gathering information** about medications, including jotting down answers to the questions noted above in the Procovery Notes for Consumers section, or doing Web research, or calling to determine health coverage for specific medications being considered.

❖ **Look to support, not enforce.** A psychiatric diagnosis is generally accompanied by a horrible feeling of loss. An added loss of autonomy can be too much to bear. Offering to serve as a medication reminder can be supportive, but trying to enforce the medication is not, especially in the long term.

❖ **Validate side effects.** Stabilizing on a medication can be extraordinarily difficult. Side effects are frequently cited as the No. 1 reason for non-compliance. Do not downplay side effects, even if they strike *you* as minimal when compared with the obvious benefit. Listen. Validate. Support.

Separate medication side effects from the disorder/person. —Rex Sibling, NAMI Sibling and Adult Children Network.[8]

❖ **During appointments, keep in mind that the consumer and health care professional are building a collaborative partnership** that can in itself have significant therapeutic value. Avoid interrupting and contradicting your relative. If something important has been misrepresented, bring it up with your loved one privately if possible. Family members may remember some things more clearly but, unless the difference is critical, talking past your relative can be damaging both to your relationship with your relative and to your loved one's initially very tenuous therapeutic relationship with his or her treating professional.

❖ **Psychiatric medications are powerful, often sedative, and difficult to stabilize**. Often a drug-induced, highly sedative effect is confused with lack of motivation, interest, or understanding. Consumers often report frustration that in day-to-day conversation, people lean closer, talk louder, repeat themselves, use exaggerated hand gestures, or talk about the consumer in front of him or her. This is something to keep in mind and possibly bring to the attention of other family members, friends, etc.

❖ **During a heat wave users of many psychotropic meds are at increased risk**. See the Procovery Note for Consumers, above.

❖ **Many medications cause weight gain, extreme fatigue, and other unpleasant side effects**, increasing frustration with an otherwise promising medication. See the Procovery Notes for Family in the chapter on "Exercising Self-Care: Actions to Take and Choices to Make."

❖ **Help with the trial period countdown**. It is challenging to remain on a medication for the full trial period. Especially when you often feel worse before you feel better. Sometimes a countdown calendar or chart that can be crossed out each day of the trial period, or a planned celebration at the end of the trial period will support the effort.

Procovery Notes for Staff

❖ **Offer choice to the fullest extent possible**—type, dosage, timing, trial period. Somewhere there must be *some* area for choice—find it and build on it.

❖ **Avoid setting false expectations**.[9] Consumers need to understand that taking psychotropic medications is frequently a trial-and-error process, both as to the medication and as to the therapeutic dosage. After trying one medication, there may need to be a medication-free period before trying another. The trial period may last weeks or months before the efficacy of a medication is known. As a result, a consumer may likely feel worse (from "side" effects) immediately and not know for some time how much of—or if—the particular medication will help. Providing realistic expectations may mean that consumers will need more support during the initial medication period, but this is likely to translate into less support in the long term.

❖ **Avoid the medication pyramid whenever possible**. Research supports that multiple medications complicate and reduce compliance, and obviously increase the risks of drug-drug interactions.[10] Explore self-care options and preventive measures, where available, before prescribing additional drugs to assist in the management of "side" effects of the primary medication. Additionally, adopt the least complicated medication schedule possible.

❖ **Agree, perhaps in writing, on a window of time to try a medication before moving on to another**. Consumers often state that their medication isn't working and it hasn't been working, and they want to try a new medication, or alter the dosage or timing. Doctors often disagree, based on their direct observations that the targeted symptoms appear to be improving, or based upon a need to give the medication more time to work. But a consumer often is not clear on what symptoms the doctor is targeting, or the measures of success, or the time frame. It would be easier all around, and would increase compliance, if there were an agreed-upon window of time, a basis for the criteria for success (listing the agreed-upon targeted symptoms), and an understanding as to the next proposed treatment if the medication is unsuccessful.

❖ **Validate and address "side" effects communicated by a consumer**. Never downplay side effects. It is incredibly disempowering for a consumer to be told that his or her description of side effects is inaccurate. Enough stigma and discrimination occur outside of the doctor's office as a result of a psychiatric diagnosis; stigma generated inside the doctor's office is obviously unproductive, untherapeutic and an obstacle to procovery. Dismissing a consumer's concerns can only succeed in communicating a lack of understanding or caring about the substantial impact of many of these "side" effects. Often listening and validating the difficulties of medication stabilization, despite the inability to alter the facts, will indicate to a consumer that the professional and consumer are at least on the same team and will increase the likelihood that the consumer will stay with the treatment through the optimum trial period despite difficult "side" effects.

❖ **When a consumer is doing well, don't automatically schedule less frequent medication checks.** Consumers who are experiencing a period of wellness are at high risk for non-compliance and relapse.[11] And yet the natural, seemingly rational reaction when consumers are doing well is to see them less frequently. Consumers and professionals both work so hard at achieving stabilization; it makes therapeutic and economic sense to continue the effort once stability is attained. Short visits can communicate the benefits and needs with regard to continued compliance with a mutually agreed-upon maintenance plan, resulting in increased compliance and reduced relapse and crisis.

❖ **Some questions for staff to ask:**

- What do you feel you need to feel better?

- Are there any medications you have had success with in the past?

- Are there any medications you have found unhelpful or problematic in the past?

- Is there anyone you would like to have accompany you for med checks, etc.?

- (After handing the prescription to a consumer) Do you plan to take this medication as prescribed?

1. Blaska, Betty (1990). "The Myriad Medication Mistakes in Psychiatry: A Consumer's View," *Hospital and Community Psychiatry*, 41, 993-998.

2. Between 1985 and 1994, the number of visits during which a psychotropic medication was prescribed increased from 32.73 million to 45.64 million. Part of this has been a significant increase in prescribing of drugs by non-psychiatrists. Pincus, H. (1998). "Prescribing Trends in Psychotropic Medications," *Journal of the American Medical Association*: 1998;279:526-531.

3. "Medication has been the single most potent force in emptying the hospitals from their highest use in the 1950s to the present. If not for the discovery of antipsychotic medications, is there any serious doubt that these hospitals would still be crammed with patients? Nothing else has made a significant difference. Civil rights cases and exposés of inhumane hospital treatment, the family movement, and mental health legislation would have had little if any effect on the mental hospital population if medication had not made it possible for the heretofore intractable mentally ill to leave those institutions successfully." Dincin, Jerry (1995). *New Directions, A Pragmatic Approach to Psychiatric Rehabilitation: Lessons from Chicago's Thresholds Program*, 1995 Winter; 68:13. For an alternate view, see Johnson, Ann Braden (1990), *Out of Bedlam: The Truth About Institutionalization*, New York: Basic Books, 38-52.

4. Styron, William (1990). *Darkness Visible: A Memoir of Madness*, New York: Random House, 54.

5. Dincin, Jerry (1995). *New Directions, A Pragmatic Approach to Psychiatric Rehabilitation: Lessons from Chicago's Thresholds Program*, 1995 Winter; 68:15.

6. Blaska, Betty (1990). "The Myriad Medication Mistakes in Psychiatry: A Consumer's View," *Hospital and Community Psychiatry*, 41, 993-998.

7. Keatinge, W.R. (1987). "Heat," *in* Weathrall, D.J., Ledingham, J.G.G., Warrell, D.A., eds., *Oxford Textbook of Medicine*, 2nd ed. London: ELBS/Oxford University Press, 6.92-6.93. *See also* Yarbrough, B. (1992), "Heat illness," *in* Rosen, P., Barkin, R.M., Braen, G.R., *et. al*, eds. *Emergency Medicine: Concepts and Clinical Practice*, 3rd ed., St. Louis: Mosby Year Book, 944-964.

8. Sibling, Rex. *60 tips on coping with mental illness in the family*. NAMI Sibling and Adult Children Network.

9. "Perhaps the major problem compromising the potential effectiveness of acute phase pharmacotherapy is attrition from treatment before receipt of an adequate trial. Attrition rates from clinical trials often are as high as 30 percent to 40 percent (Depression Guideline Panel, 1993). And although side effects are a principal factor,

such non-adherence may also be attributable to inadequate psychoeducation (resulting in unrealistic expectations about pharmacotherapy), ambivalence about taking medication and practical roadblocks (e.g., the cost or accessibility of services)." Thase, M. and Kupfer, D., "Recent Developments in the Pharmacotherapy of Mood Disorders." *Journal of Consulting and Clinical Psychology*, 1996: 64(4): 646-659.

10. Goodwin, Frederick, M.D. (1996). "Current Concepts in Treating Bi-Polar Disorder," *Journal of Clinical Psychiatry Intercom*, March 1996 (discussion format).*Also see* Blaska, Betty (1990). "The Myriad Medication Mistakes in Psychiatry: A Consumer's View," *Hospital and Community Psychiatry*, 41, 993-998.

11. Tohen, Mauricio, M.D. (1996). "Current Concepts in Treating Bi-Polar Disorder," *Journal of Clinical Psychiatry Intercom*, March 1996 (discussion format).

Uncovering Hope

Hope is the thing with feathers
That perches in the soul
And sings the tune without the words
And never stops at all.
And sweetest in the gale is heard;
And sore must be the storm
That could abash the little bird
That kept so many warm.
I've heard it in the chillest land
And on the strangest sea,
Yet never in extremity
It asked a crumb of me.

—Emily Dickinson

It is hopelessness even more than pain that crushes the soul. —William Styron, *Darkness Visible*

K.H. Litrell writes, "The analysis of hope in individuals with severe and persistent mental illness is conspicuously absent from the literature."[1] This is a terrible mistake, in that hope is a tangible and essential ingredient in procovery.

The Criticality of Hope to Procovery: Hope is the Answer to the Question, "WHY?"

He who has a why to live for can bear with almost any how. —Friedrich Nietzsche

Individuals diagnosed with chronic mental illness are often handed a treatment plan that is incredibly difficult to follow and a very bleak picture of what is possible for them.

Breaking the seemingly endless cycle of chronic illness is hard work. With no vision for the future, with no sense of hope, why do it?

Proverbs 29:18 states, "Where there is no vision, the people perish." Simplistically speaking and most important, hope is the answer to the question, "WHY?"

- WHY get out of bed in the morning?

- WHY work harder than you have ever worked to feel worse than you ever knew it was possible to feel?

- WHY take a medication that is likely to make you feel worse immediately and only possibly help you feel better in the future?

- WHY take three buses clear across town to interview for a rooming house in a violent, crime-ridden neighborhood?

- And WHY apply for a job where, even if you get it, you will be paid minimally, stigmatized maximally, and risk losing your benefits?

In order to get up every day, put one foot in front of the other, and wade through the living hell of mental illness— toward the not-so-visible light at the end of the very dark tunnel, toward procovery, there HAS TO BE some sense that things can somehow work out.

Integrating Hope and Health: The Biology of Hope

Positive emotions create positive reactions in the body, and negative emotions create negative reactions.[2] The biology of this may be in dispute, but the fact of it is not; hope is an enormous factor in healing.

Some say the therapeutic benefit of hope is unproved and unscientific. In fact, hope is researched in double blind study after double blind study funded by every pharma-ceutical firm and countless agencies and universities. These studies just put a different name on the bottle: they call it a placebo. It is commonly cited that placebo effects account for about 33 percent of treatment effectiveness, and a study by Dr. Alan Roberts based on results from almost 7,000 patients indicates that placebo effects in clinical situations may be as high as 70 percent when both doctors and patients believe that a treatment will be effective.[3]

Integrating Hope and Treatment Services: Hope is the Engine of Motivation

Hope is not yet widely embraced as a treatment technique or objective. Frequently it is thought of as a waste of time, unscientific, and dangerous, something that can create false expectations and lead to profound disappointment. Overworked and time-compromised staff have enough to do—what with helping consumers stabilize on a medication, addressing side effects and non-compliance, dealing with crises, and including family members in the information equation. In other words, staff are generally dealing with all-too-concrete, everyday needs to be dispensing hope in addition—or so some think.

Yet lack of motivation is often cited by staff as a major impediment to successful treatment. A common refrain is, "People with serious mental illness don't need 'hope'; they need serious solutions—medications, therapy, housing, money, jobs. They need to become motivated and compliant."

Conversely, consumers often cite lack of hope as a devastating impediment to healing. "It's like being in hell, with no hope of leaving and no memory of being anywhere different." If you believe that nothing you do will help, then you are unlikely to do anything.

Without hope, motivation is enormously difficult. With hope, motivation is a short step. In this sense, hope is the engine of motivation.

Any treatment of an illness that does not minister to the human spirit is grossly deficient. —Jerome D. Frank

There is a word for motivation based on hope, and that word is *inspiration*. Rudolph Steiner, paraphrasing William Yeats, once said about education that "the goal is not to fill a bucket but to light a fire." This pertains to the treatment of serious mental illness as well. The need is not just to fill a bucket by providing clinical and rehabilitation services, but to light a fire by rebuilding dreams, a reason to be.

At the essence of procovery is an approach, with hope as its core. Sometimes a single hope-building action will plant a seed, making a lifetime of difference; and sometimes just knowing enough to avoid a hope-busting statement can prevent a spiral of despair.

A hopeful, inspiring attitude toward the experience of chronic mental illness can be dispensed in conjunction with any other aspect of a treatment plan, at no material economic cost and at a substantial therapeutic benefit.

What Hope Is, and What Hope Is Not

What is hope?

There is an excellent definition of hope given by James Gordon, M.D., who says that hope is the name we give to the feeling that things might somehow work out. This simple statement best captures in my view the expectation that is central to procovery.

It is useful to differentiate hoping from wishing. Wishing is passive, merely *wanting* an outcome; hoping is when you want an outcome *and expect that you might get it.*

Wish / vb: to have a desire
Hope / vb: to cherish a desire with expectation of fulfillment[4]

Hope is *active*. Hope as it relates to procovery focuses on what you can do, with what you have, now.[5]

Appetite, with an opinion of attaining, is called hope; the same, without such opinion, despair. —Thomas Hobbes

The following anecdote illustrates the difference between passive wishing and concrete, active hoping:

> Sheldon dies. Upon entrance to heaven, he asks God in a passionate, questioning manner, 'Why, after all these years of praying, every single day, that I might win the lottery, not even once did you allow me to win? Not even a dollar!' God answers, in an equally passionate and questioning manner, 'Just tell me, Sheldon, why, after all those years, not even once did you ever help out and buy a lottery ticket?'

Growing Hope

Hope, like some basic force of nature, seems to live stubbornly, if barely perceptibly, inside even the most depressed of us, waiting like some sleeping beauty for the faintest

glimmer of light, the slightest sympathetic touch, to awaken it. We should cherish hope.
—James Gordon, M.D.[6]

Hope is a seed that is always there. But it is often difficult to grow hope until you understand where hope exists, where it is missing, and where it has been crushed so many times that it is reluctant to appear again.

For us giving up was a way of surviving. Giving up, refusing to hope, not trying, not caring; all of these were ways of trying to protect the last fragile traces of our spirit and our selfhood from undergoing another crushing.
—Patricia Deegan, Ph.D.[7]

Where can you find an individual's seeds of hope?

Sometimes, you can look at an individual's actions. People are unlikely to take action where they perceive the situation as hopeless. In fact, if someone is doing *anything* to impact the quality of his or her life, that person is probably hopeful to some degree, whether others might view it as small-scale (getting out of bed, taking a shower, attending a doctor's appointment) or large-scale (changing meds, voluntarily entering a psychiatric hospital, applying for a job, finding a new place to live, starting an exercise program). Those actions can be starting points for growing hope further.

And sometimes you can ask questions to gain an understanding not only of where hope is lacking but also of where it might begin to grow. For example: What did you dream before you stopped dreaming? What did you used to like to do? What would you like to do now?

Hope Building vs. Hope Busting

We have been taught to believe that negative equals realistic and positive equals unrealistic. —Susan Jeffers

Frustrations and experience may lead professionals to deliver not hope but instead the scientific safety net called "realistic expectations." And in the absence of concrete evidence of the future, staff may focus on what they are trained to do best—to analyze the present.

In my own treatment, even after I was labeled as physically and mentally disabled for life, every week I'd hear a new observation or diagnosis or acquire a new label. Some new problem, or weakness, or area of concern would be noticed, and it would become the focus of that office visit.

I later saw a New Yorker cartoon that quite accurately depicts how I began to feel (see next page).

My hopes were dashed constantly with remarks like:

- We're doing all we can, your case is very complicated. There's just nothing else to try.

- I could definitely have helped if I'd seen you sooner, but now that scar tissue has formed, I'm afraid there is nothing we can do about your pain or depression. It's too late now.

"Hmm—I don't like the looks of that eye"

- You've got to reduce your stress. Between your poor physical and mental health, and financial and marital problems, research indicates with your level of stress you're likely to develop cancer within five years.

- You're just wasting your time and money looking into alternative therapies. They don't work!

- Why are you trying to kick your illness under the rug by denying it? We can make you comfortable with morphine and anti-depressants and get you on disability. Why are you looking further?

Hope busters come in all forms. They can be professionals, consumers, or family members. And they can crush hope in all of us, whether professional, consumer, or family member.

My message about dealing with hope busters is simple—*stay away from them.*

Some people can stay longer in an hour than others can in a week. —William Dean Howells

On the other side are hope builders. What might hope builders say?

- It never hurts to try.

- We learn more every day.

- There's not one answer. Individuals respond differently to different treatments. And even to the same treatment over a period of time.

- It's a matter of finding what works for you.

- Let's find some things you might enjoy that *are* still available to you.

- It will get better. I see you as the type of person that will make it get better.

- Together we'll give it a shot.

- And perhaps my favorite one of all—even if no one has ever licked this, why can't you be the first?

The choice to bust or build hope is within the power of the individual, over and over again, in *every single interaction.*

About Hope Building

When one door closes another opens. But we often look so long and so regretfully upon the closed door that we fail to see the one that has opened for us.
—Helen Keller

Sometimes we are so specific in our thinking about hope that it is self-limiting. Sometimes we hope so long and so hard for one specific thing that we don't notice or take advantage of other hopeful opportunities that present themselves.

> *There was a farmer at the time of a great flood. When the waters got to the farmer's bottom windows, a neighbor rowed over to rescue him. The farmer declined, 'I'm a man of faith. God will rescue me.' When the water rose to the second-story windows, another neighbor appeared in a motorboat. Again the farmer declined to be rescued, 'I'm a man of faith. God will save me.' Finally, as the farmer sat on his roof, a helicopter flew over and lowered a ladder. Once again the farmer declined, 'I'm a man of faith. I'm certain that God will save me.' The next thing he knew, the farmer found himself at the pearly gates. 'What happened?' he moaned to Saint Peter. 'Why didn't God save me?' Saint Peter shook his head sadly, saying, 'Listen here, we sent a rowboat, a motorboat, and a helicopter!'*
> —Joan Borysenko

The best medication, health care practitioner, CSP program, clubhouse, supported employment program, or any other rehabilitative effort operates at half force, at best, if hope is not dispensed in conjunction.[8]

Procovery Notes for Consumers

❖ **Remember to Just Start Anywhere**. If you don't feel like doing jobs one through seven on your personal task list, it's OK. Choose any action that gets you moving forward positively, in any increment.

Focus on life rather than illness, on strengths rather than weaknesses. It has been said that learning to draw is learning to see; learning procovery is learning to recognize and build upon what *is* available in life.

❖ **Rather than looking backward, look forward**. Instead of asking, "Why did this happen? What could I have done to prevent it? What did I do to deserve it?" ask, "What can I do about it? What can I do to move forward?"

❖ **Sometimes in the face of illness our dreams blow up in our face**. Dream a new dream, and once you've done this pick some aspect of it and begin working toward it in any increment.

Imagination is the beginning of creation. You imagine what you desire; you will what you imagine; and at last you create what you will. —George Bernard Shaw

The greatest achievement was at first and for a time a dream. —James Allen

❖ **Keep in mind that statistics are not facts**. Statistics frequently can predict how one million people will vote in an election, but they can't predict how you will vote. Similarly, although statistics can describe the effects of treatments on broad populations of consumers, no statistic can determine how *you* will heal.

Use statistics to select the best treatment approach, but then throw statistics aside—they have nothing to say about your individual outcome.

So if depression is a frequent side effect of a particular medication, and you are prone to depression, by all means seek an alternative treatment. But if you are told that 95 percent of people who have an illness with which you are diagnosed die within five years, who is to say that you aren't one of the 5 percent? Further, as Dr. Bernie Siegel has said, "Even if no one has ever licked your particular illness, why can't you be the first?"

Do not put faith in what statistics say until you have carefully considered what they do not say.
—William W. Watt

◈ **Accept backsliding**. Procovery can be two steps forward, one back—or sometimes one step forward and two back. We all have our good and bad days, procovering individuals included. Backsliding is a natural part of the procovery process. In addition, sometimes backsliding provides information as to what didn't work.

You may have to fight a battle more than once to win it. —Margaret Thatcher

❖ **Some people will give you energy. Some will take it away**. The former are better. Be careful of the "hope busters" and "energy vacuums" out there who will suck you dry if you let them.

❖ **Don't box your hope in by limiting it to one specific outcome**. You often succeed in ways that are incremental, or that you hadn't planned.

❖ **Look for books, movies, and music that trigger hope for you**.

❖ **Fake it 'til you make it**. The mere act of pretending or acting as if we were feeling better than we actually feel has been shown to move us physically in this direction.

If you have no enthusiasm, put on a front. Act enthusiastic, and the feeling will become genuine.
—Rabbi Nachman, a late 18th century Jewish mystic

If you want a quality, act as if you already had it. Try the 'as if' technique. —William James

❖ **Find out what pulls rather than pushes you**. Go where the positive energy is.

Don't worry about what the world wants from you, worry about what makes you come more alive. Because what the world really needs are people who are more alive. —Lawrence LeShan

❖ **Help others**. In his book, "The Healing Power of Doing Good," Allan Luks describes the healing benefit of helping others. It is easy to be consumed by our own lives, but important to remember that reaching out to others can heal—others as well as ourselves.

Happiness is a perfume you cannot pour on others without getting a few drops on yourself.
—Ralph Waldo Emerson

The way to be happy is to make others so.
—Robert Ingersoll

❖ **Find a plot of dirt to start a garden**, take a walk in a local park, feed the ducks, volunteer at a food pantry, try a new recipe. If you have no reason to get out of bed, you're less likely to do so. The most "therapeutic" activities are generally the ones we escape into, losing our sense of time, consumed by what we are doing.

❖ **Remind yourself that new research is always being done** and new treatments are always in development.

❖ **Celebrate—often—your efforts**. Mark your improvements, whether they seem big or small.

❖ **Keep a hope journal** you write in when you are happy and hopeful, and read it when you are not.

❖ **Create a hope box**, with reminders of things that build hope—photos, quotes, etc.—and reminders of things that bust hope.

❖ **Keep handy a list of hope builders to call**, and hope busters not to call.

❖ **The first thing every morning**—and the last thing every night—ask yourself, "What's good in my life?"

Procovery Notes for Family Members

❖ **Fake it 'til you make it**. The mere act of pretending or acting as if we are feeling hopeful can move us physically in this direction.

❖ **Keep in mind that, at one time, there was no vaccine for cholera**, or treatment for tuberculosis or gonorrhea. Smallpox has been virtually eradicated. New research is always being done and new treatments are always in development.

❖ **Recognize backsliding as the natural rhythm of progress**. Procovery is highly individual and excruciatingly difficult. There is no one path, and finding the right path means trying all kinds of things. Backsliding may be an indication that your relative is facing the challenge. Remember the enormous difficulty of the challenge, and try to be particularly supportive in the slump periods.

◈ **Whether it's two steps forward and one step back,** or one step forward and two steps back, celebrate the steps forward.

◈ **Learn to let go of what was, and revel in what is.**

◈ **Don't fall into a trap of feeling hopeful on days your loved one is doing well, and unhopeful on the bad days or times.** This can create its own negative cycle, just the opposite of what you and your loved one need.

There are two ways of spreading light: to be the candle or the mirror that reflects it. —Edith Wharton

◈ **Recognize that hope is as critical as any other part of the treatment plan.**

◈ **Look for books, movies, music that trigger hope** not only for your loved one but for you!

◈ **When things are going well for your loved one,** ask and make note of what represents or stirs or builds hope, and what crushes it.

◈ **Put hope triggers around your house.** Make quite visible "happy" memories, such as photos, souvenirs, "remember that day" kind of stuff. Your goal is not to create a mausoleum to a no longer available past— reflections of times that are no longer available, old trophies and memories—but instead to go for the laughing photo from last week's family dinner.

Procovery Notes for Staff

❖ **To paraphrase Herbert Kohl writing about education, adopt a "discipline of hope"**—a refusal to accept limits on how far individuals can procover, and on what you as a healer can do to facilitate their procovery.

Unexpected healing happens often enough that physicians must learn to project hope at all times, even in what seem to be the final hours. Patients are not looking for the results of a medical Gallup poll. They are looking for a success-oriented relationship.
—Bernie Siegel, M.D.

❖ **Plant a seed of hope or kindness, without expectations on an outcome**. You never know which seed will sprout when. Consumers often tell stories about their process of procovery beginning years after a kind staff member planted a seed.

❖ **Take advantage of the ripple effect to grow hope**. Whether it is your hopeful words or attitude, or the hopeful materials you recommend, or your putting consumers or families in touch with others who have been there and made it through, you have the ability to help hope grow exponentially.

Scatter joy. —Ralph Waldo Emerson

❖ **Look for ways to grow your own hope**. Talk to other staff members, or to consumers; keep your eye out for hope-building materials and individuals.

❖ **Keep in mind that hope is fuel for healing.**

Humans are time-binding creatures, so assumptions about the future have a powerful effect on one's state.
—Jerome Frank

❖ **Generally, people would rather be inspired than motivated.** Rather than focusing on motivating individuals, try to inspire them.

❖ **If you have no reason to get out of bed in the morning, you're less likely to do so.** Help identify a reason.

❖ **Ask the question, "What do you find particularly hopeful (or depressing)?"** In crises, ask, "What do you have to live for?"

❖ **Comment when you note improvement,** no matter how slight it appears to you.

❖ **Communicate that statistics are descriptive, not predictive.**

Physicians must stop letting statistics determine their beliefs. Statistics are important when one is choosing the best therapy for a certain illness, but once that choice is made, they no longer apply to the individual. All individuals must be accorded the conviction that they can get well no matter what the odds.
—Bernie Siegel, M.D.

❖ **Accept backsliding**. It is unrealistic with a serious illness to expect that consumers will move only forward. Anything constantly moving forward is likely moving downhill.

❖ **Ask, "What did you dream about before you stopped dreaming?"**

When you cease to dream, you cease to live.
—Malcolm Forbes

❖ **Maintain compassion.**

A warm smile and an outstretched hand were valued even above the offerings of modern science, but the latter were far more accessible than the former. I believe that nothing a hospital could provide in the way of technological marvels was as helpful as an atmosphere of compassion. —Norman Cousins

❖ **Remember to Just Start Anywhere.**

---

1. Littrell, K.H., Herth, K.A., & Hinteh, L.E. (1996). "The Experience of Hope in Adults with Schizophrenia," *Psychiatric Rehabilitation Journal*, 19(4), 61-65.

2. Dr. O. Carl Simonton, in his work on cancer, describes the physiological pathways by which feelings can impact biology to create health. He suggests that the hypothalamus, a small area in the brain, receives input from the limbic system which among other things records stress and its effects. The hypothalamus participates in controlling the immune system and also plays a critical role in regulating the activity of the pituitary gland, which in turn regulates the reminder of the endocrine system with its vast range of hormonal control functions throughout the body. See Simonton, O. Carl, M.D.

(1978). *Getting Well Again*, New York: Bantam Books, p. 91-99.

3. Roberts, Alan, M.D. (1995). "The Powerful Placebo Revisited: Magnitude of Nonspecific Effects," *Mind/Body Medicine*, March 1995, Vol. 1 No. 1 p. 35.

4. *Webster's New Encyclopedic Dictionary*, Black Dog and Leventhal Publishing, p. 479 (definition of hope), p. 1196 (definition of wish).

5. Credit to Theodore Roosevelt, who said, "Do what you can, with what you have, now."

6. Gordon, James, M.D. (1996). *Manifesto for a New Medicine*, New York: Addison-Wesley Publishing Co., 286.

7. Deegan, P.E. (1994). "A letter to my friend who is giving up," *The Journal of the California Alliance for the Mentally Ill*, 5, p. 19.

8. "Findings indicate that increased levels of hope in individuals with schizophrenia may be associated with improvement in symptoms. Diminished symptoms and increased hopefulness, in turn, were felt to enhance treatment interventions and improve reintegration outcomes." Littrell, K.H., Herth, K.A., and Hinteh, L.E. (1996). "The Experience of Hope in Adults with Schizophrenia," *Psychiatric Rehabilitation Journal*, 19(4), 61-65.

Creating Change

They always say time changes things, but you actually have to change them yourself. —Andy Warhol

Most people are consuming so much time and energy trying to do the impossible—namely, to change and control the actions of OTHERS—that they wrongly believe that they cannot do the one thing that is most possible—to change themselves. —Albert Ellis (paraphrased)[1]

In order for a person to procover, all kinds of changes need to take place. Learning to look forward rather than back, focusing on strengths rather than weaknesses, focusing on life rather than illness. Procovery is a highly individual path toward finding what works for you.

Change is a given on the path to procovery, yet change can be scary. Change involves taking a chance and rocking the boat. You think maybe things could be better, but at the same time you *know* they could be worse. You might remember your darkest depression, or paralyzing sense of isolation, or you might remember awakening heavily medicated and being told how out of control and psychotic you were. You might remember being locked up against your will, or being forcibly medicated, or being picked up by the police.

Then, too, fear of the unknown future can be a major stumbling block as well. Sometimes we feel, as my grandma used to say, "Better the devil you know than the devil you don't."

Change can be lonely. Those who innovate, those who look past the status quo frequently do so only by looking past the questioning and bemusement of others. Change in one person can be a source of insecurity and fear in those close to them.

The other terror that scares us from self-trust is our consistency; a reverence for our past act or word because the eyes of others have no other data for computing our orbit than our past acts, and we are loath to disappoint them.
—Ralph Waldo Emerson

And change can be a fight uphill. When you're already in significant pain, the process of moving forward, especially given the uncertainty of outcome, can seem interminable and insurmountable.

But fear can be used to prepare for the process of change, and the momentum of incremental steps can make it happen.

Overcoming Fear

Heroes are those who move forward, not without fear, but without succumbing to their fear. —Erich Fromm[2]

It can help to think of overcoming fear as a two-step process: *analyze* and *prepare*.

Analyzing fear involves recognizing that fear can some-times become mixed up with positive emotions such as excitement, anticipation, and courage. One approach that can be helpful in separating these emotions is to analyze the change or action for *unreasonable risk*; that is, explore the down side. In this way, fear of a roller coaster for many of us will have significantly greater amounts of excitement and anticipation—and therefore might be more readily overcome—than, for example, cliff-diving. Just as with prescribing a medication where the potential gains are weighed against the risks, overcoming fear becomes partially an assessment of gains and risks.

In order to analyze fear of a specific change, it might help to ask questions such as: If I do this:

- What's the most likely outcome?

- What's the worst thing that could happen?

- How likely is that to happen?

- What's the best thing that could happen?

- What's the likelihood of this happening?

- What if I don't do this?

Life is change—whether it's a promotion at work, the death of a loved one, school graduation, a natural disaster, an inheritance, or a new romance. We can either allow these changes to happen to us, or we can climb into the driver's seat and decide how we will anticipate, seek out, and react to these changes.

When you have to make a choice and don't make it, that is in itself a choice. —William James

Preparing for fear is the second step. Preparation puts fear to work as a tool, driving us to ensure that we maximally prepare for change.

Fear of speaking publicly is a common phobia, and one that I shared. The first time I agreed to speak in front of a large group, I was terrified. What pulled me through was my father's advice. He validated my fear, but recommended I use it—to prepare. Write (and rewrite and rewrite) the best speech I could, and practice it daily. By the time I finally gave the speech, I was surprisingly calm because I had used the fear to prepare scrupulously.

There are many ways that individuals diagnosed with mental illness can prepare for the changes that they will encounter on the path to procovery—building a personal safety net or support system, finding a way to test the waters, taking smaller steps. What is wonderful about any preparation is that it pays double dividends: first, it helps the change become successful, and second, it increases feelings of self-confidence and self-efficacy.

When a person brings about actual change, he or she increases feelings of mastery and control. This, in turn, leads to further and more effective change.
—Judy Chamberlin[3]

Overcoming fear is not done in a single action or a single moment; it is a continual process. But it can get easier over time, as the fears become based less on what is today than on what was.

And then when fears re-emerge, the central question can be asked: *What is different now?* In what way are you now prepared, that you weren't before? Do you have support in place that you didn't before? Are you stabilized on a medication? Do you now have a collaborative relationship with a professional? These differences can serve as a reminder of why you need not succumb to those fears.

Creating Momentum

A single day is enough to make us a little larger or, another time, a little smaller. —Paul Klee

Creating momentum can be an extraordinarily helpful part of creating change. If you've ever tried to push a car on a level street, you know that the momentum you create makes continued movement easier. Similarly, the momentum of change can create its own energy, simplifying further change. Strategies for creating this momentum include:

- **Seek incremental change**. Change is not necessarily a matter of taking large steps but of taking any steps, no matter how small they might seem.

  A journey of a thousand miles begins with a single step. —Lao-tzu

- **Don't assume you need to wait for more information, to stabilize on a med, to complete a treatment regimen, to make any effective change**. Erich Fromm writes in *The Art of Listening*, "Psychoanalysis has the great danger that everything is put under analysis and that people believe only when the analysis is over, is finished, then will they make the changes. I am convinced that one has to begin making changes before, and the question is only what changes and the problem of graduality, and the quality of changes one can make—changes which are not unrealistic, which don't go beyond one's capacity to make them at the moment."

- **Be inspired by the potential for change to make a difference not just in the distant future, but now**. I remember being in a psychiatric ward and receiving a letter from my sister in which she wrote, "I talked to Mama last night and she told me about your therapy and repeated that line I hate—'It took a long time for you to get into this condition, so it will take a long time for you to get out.' Piffle. I know a man that went through years of therapy and several operations in order to walk again after an auto accident that happened in the space of a few moments. Then there are adults who have been blind all of their lives and gain their sight after an operation—quite suddenly. There's no necessary connection between the time it takes to get into a mess and the time it takes to get out again."

This inspired me. I was tired of hearing how long a haul it was going to be, tired of hearing that slow, incremental change was the best I could reach for, the best I could expect. I was tired of being asked to be reasonable and rational in my expectations. I wanted to feel better, and soon.

- **Change bad habits by replacing them with positive habits**. One of the hardest changes is to break bad habits. One approach is to "just stop doing it"; this can be the hardest route to take. An approach often taken but not recommended is to replace an old bad habit with a new bad habit. Instead consider trading an old bad habit for a new good one, one that both substitutes *and reinforces* the change. Examples: You might decide to stop eating so much candy and decide to eat more fruits and vegetables. Or to stop sleeping so late and decide to volunteer at the local hospital each morning. Or to stop drinking alcohol to relax and decide to start relaxation techniques. Or to stop doing drugs and hanging around drug-addicted friends, and decide to join a new support group and go to church. Or to stop holding your anger in and start journaling. Or to stop drinking coffee each morning and decide to start drinking green tea each morning instead. Or to stop using your credit card because you are in debt and decide to take a money management course.

Autobiography in Five Short Chapters
by Portia Nelson

Chapter One
I walk down the street
There is a deep hole in the sidewalk
I fall in.
I am lost . . . I am helpless.
It isn't my fault.
It takes forever to find a way out.

Chapter Two
I walk down the same street.
There is a deep hole in the sidewalk
I pretend I don't see it.
I fall in again.
I can't believe I am in this same place.
But, it isn't my fault.
It still takes a long time to get out.

Chapter Three
I walk down the same street.

There is a deep hole in the sidewalk.

I see it is there.

I still fall in . . . it's a habit . . . but,

My eyes are open.

I know where I am.

It is *my* fault.

Chapter Four

I walk down the same street.

There is a deep hole in the sidewalk.

I walk around it.

Chapter Five

I walk down another street.

• **Focus on what you can affect**. Change that leads to procovery can focus not on the complexities of the illness, but instead on what can be affected in the rest of one's life. Psychiatrist Lee Jones once offered me this analogy: "Imagine, Kathleen, you have a house, and it's a fine house. But it has this big ugly tree growing right up there through the middle of it. And you don't have the option of moving. And you can't get rid of the tree. What would you do?" "Well," I said, "I guess I would make the rest of the house as beautiful as possible so that the tree was not the focus." That tree represented physical and emotional pain to me—but what about the rest of the house? It was that day that I stopped reaching to recover in the traditional sense, stopped reaching to regain a former state of health, stopped reaching to be the person I used to be.[4]

Like procovery itself, creating change is an individual choice of how best to move forward. There are no rules as to whether change must be a roar or a whisper, whether it must be one step or one of a hundred steps, or whether it takes a moment or a year. It does take courage, but, in this variability, there is enormous freedom to procover and to become.

I have become a new person; and those who knew the old person laughed at me. The only man who behaved sensibly was my tailor. He took my measure anew every time he saw me, while all the rest went on with their old measurements and expected me to fit. —George Bernard Shaw

Procovery Notes for Consumers

◈ **Change can be scary**. Validate and accept your fears—don't beat yourself up for feeling afraid.

◈ **Assess whether the fear is a message that you shouldn't do something**, or is the fear something you should work through.

The fearful person does not care whether his model is accurate. What he wants is to feel safe. He wants a model that is reassuring, simple, unchanging . . . On the principle that you can't fall out of bed if you're sleeping on the floor; you can't lose any money if you don't place any bets. —John Holt[5]

❖ **Develop a destination and follow through**—plan your work and work your plan.

The alternative to creating what we most want, is to endure whatever we get. —Simple Living Network

❖ **Use fear to improve preparation**. Suppose you are interested in attending a support group but you feel nervous doing so. Inquire as to whether you could just observe at the first meeting. Or suppose there is someone you are interested in dating but you are uncomfortable asking him or her out. Consider as a first step arranging a group gathering and including your desired date. Or suppose you are interested in but fearful of getting a full-time job because you are not sure how it would affect your health. You might test the waters by volunteering for a defined period of time at the same schedule you would be working.

Courage is mastery of fear—not absence of fear.
—Mark Twain

❖ **When past fears surface, remind yourself how your current situation might be different from the past**—your medications, your support, your lifestyle, your preparation, etc. Even if nothing is any different, when you look at the prospect of revisiting your worst-case scenario, it can help to remember that you did make it through this once before.

◈ **Remember that change in one person can be a source of fear and insecurity in those close to them**. Because of this, change can feel lonely, as others question or even denounce the idea of change or taking a risk. Helping those close to you understand what you are doing, why, and that you still love and value them may help them and help you. All relationships and people change over time. Growing doesn't have to mean growing apart.

That's the risk you take if you change: that people you've been involved with won't like the new you. But other people who do will come along. —Lisa Alther

◈ **Move forward in small ways or big ways**. You decide how you want to begin the process of change. Remember that sometimes the smallest change is the biggest step.

Sometimes when I consider what tremendous consequences come from little things, I am tempted to think there are no little things. —Bruce Barton

◈ **Consider, rather than just trying to break an old habit cold turkey, replacing an old bad habit with a new good habit**. Many examples for doing so are in the text of this chapter.

◈ **Many times people say their biggest regrets are the things they didn't do rather than the mistakes they made**. Ask yourself how you will feel years from now, if you don't try something.

❖ **Most people do the same things in the same situation over and over and over again.** Deciding to respond to a situation in an entirely new way can break a pattern. Be creative. If there is someone you particularly admire, think about (or if you know the person, ask) how he or she would handle the situation.

❖ **Preserve the power of momentum.** On the theory of "if you want a job done, ask a busy person," no matter how small the increments, the more you do often the more you can do.

❖ **Open yourself up to change.** Sometimes, rather than tackling an area of difficulty or a specific goal, it can help to find simple, interesting ways to do everyday things differently. Try a new coffee shop or a new kind of coffee. Take a new route to an old place. Respond to a situation in a non-automated way. Brainstorm new ways for doing old things. Shake it up—change brings change.

True life is lived when tiny changes occur.
—Leo Tolstoy

Procovery Notes for Family

❖ **Listen.** Sometimes fears subside simply by being expressed and heard.

◈ **After listening to fears, consider a gentle reminder as to why things might work out better now than in the past** (e.g., stabilization on a med, a new doctor, membership in a support group, etc.).

◈ **Express support, often.**

◈ **Accept hats and suspenders.** It is a natural tendency to be more supportive of some change than we are of others; and to support differently the identical change in different people. So if a friend suddenly starts wearing hats or suspenders, we might view him as a character; but if he is our business partner we might see him as losing his edge and worry how it impacts us; and if he is an elderly person and there is a history of dementia in the family, we might view the change as evidence of an oncoming problem.

◈ **Accept and support changes in ideas and attitudes.** People often accept changes in *actions*, but when someone changes his or her *mind* (opinions, preferences, goals, etc.), people view it is a sign of being wishy-washy or weak. In procovery, where finding one's path is at least equally an internal process, changing one's mind can be a sign of strength, a sign of motivation and exploration.

A foolish consistency is the hobgoblin of little minds, adored by little statesmen and philosophers and divines. With consistency a great soul has simply noth-

ing to do. He may as well concern himself with his shadow on the wall. Speak what you think now in hard words and tomorrow speak what tomorrow thinks in hard words again, though it contradict every thing you said today.—"Ah, so you shall be sure to be misunderstood."—Is it so bad then to be misunderstood? Pythagoras was misunderstood, and Socrates, and Jesus, and Luther, and Copernicus, and Galileo, and Newton, and every pure and wise spirit that ever took flesh. —Ralph Waldo Emerson

❖ **Respect the natural rhythms of procovery.**
Procovery is not linear, but often two steps forward, and one back. It can be gliding or falling flat and climbing up again. An individual who keeps changing isn't necessarily flitzy or lacking follow-through; that individual may be evidencing tremendous courage in finding his or her own path to procovery.

❖ **Change that is going to stick is going to stem from desire.** Help find, build, and support individual desire.

Your family member is entitled to his own life journey, as you are.—Rex Sibling, NAMI Sibling and Adult Children Network[6]

Procovery Notes for Staff

❖ **Recognize and validate how scary change can be.** Follow up by gently suggesting or reminding how exciting change can be, too.

Change means movement. Movement means friction. Only in the frictionless vacuum of a nonexistent abstract world can movement or change occur without that abrasive friction of conflict. —Saul Alinsky

❖ **When considering changing a treatment plan**, strongly assess together projected gains over losses. If a consumer believes that a certain aspect of the treatment plan that you wish to change has been essential to his healing process, give weight to that judgment. Even if you feel that belief is no more accurate than a lucky penny, recognize the therapeutic power of belief and the individual nature of procovery. In addition, the smallest veering from a plan that is finally working can be terrifying. To recommend this for only a small gain may be counterproductive.

❖ **Look for ways of getting people out of the vortex of the mental health community** and open to the non-mental health world—increasing the world rather than shrinking it.

❖ **Accept and support changes in ideas and attitudes**. See this Procovery Note for Family Members, above.

❖ **Help individuals to dream a new dream, or uncover an old dream**. Even if this dream seems to you to be impossible to achieve, it is likely that the first steps to be taken for the dream may be the same first steps to be taken for *any number* of paths forward —and the dream may provide the meaning, the fuel necessary to get out of bed in the morning and put one foot in front of the other day after day.

I have had dreams and I have had nightmares. I overcame the nightmares because of my dreams. —Jonas Salk

❖ **Respect the natural rhythms of procovery**. See this Procovery Note for Family Members, above.

❖ **Evaluate and appreciate change on an individual basis**. Rather than measuring success by a specific perfect outcome, it can help to weigh today's actions against those of three months ago. One psychiatrist I know has a remarkable ability to do this. He will say quite positively, "You know, he's showing up for appointments more often these days." Or, "She's beginning to take her medications on an almost regular basis."

One has to look for the experiences and particularly resistances which a person has in making the next step, in acting differently. Otherwise one remains somewhat in an unreal situation, in spite of all the subjective experiences one has. What these changes are depends entirely on the situation. —Erich Fromm

Creating Change

---

1. Ellis, Albert (1971). *A Guide to Rational Living*, Hollywood California: Wilshire Books, 125.

2. Fromm, Erich (1996, c1976) . *To Have or To Be*, New York : Continuum, 96.

3. Chamberlin, Judy (1997). "A working definition of empowerment," *Psychiatric Rehabilitation Journal*, 20(4), 45.

4. Crowley, Kathleen (1996). *The Day Room: A Memoir of Madness and Mending*, San Francisco: Kennedy Carlisle Publishing Co.

5. Holt, John (1970). *What Do I Do on Monday?* New York: Dell Publishing, 34.

6. Sibling, Rex. *60 Tips on Coping with Mental Illness in the Family*. NAMI Sibling and Adult Children Network.

Dissolving Stigma

The barriers brought about by being placed in the category of 'mentally ill' can be overwhelming. These disadvantages include loss of rights and equal opportunities, and discrimination in employment and housing, as well as barriers created by the system's attempts at helping—e.g., lack of opportunities for self-determination, disempowering treatment practices. —William Anthony, Ph.D.[1]

Curiously enough, it was [my psychiatrist] who told me once or twice during our sessions (and after I had rather hesitantly broached the possibility of hospitalization) that I should try to avoid the hospital at all costs, owing to the stigma I might suffer. Such a comment seemed then, as it does now, extremely misguided; I had thought psychiatry had advanced long beyond the point where stigma was attached to any aspect of mental illness, including the hospital. —William Styron[2]

The stigma surrounding mental illness not only affects consumers, their families, and treating professionals, but it also has a significant impact on the cost of treatment and the economics of public assistance.

Misinformation and the Cost of Stigma

Much of this stigma is based upon misinformation and myths, including that a mental disorder is a personal flaw rather than a physical illness,[3] that mentally ill people pose a significant risk of violence,[4] and that mentally ill people are inferior, flawed, dirty, unpredictable, and unmotivated.[5]

One of the most widely believed and most damaging myths is that mental illness is a personal failure, not a physical disease. Nothing could be further from the truth.
—Tipper Gore[6]

The fear and ignorance surrounding mental illness create huge barriers in the way of procovering individuals, including discrimination in housing, education, jobs,[7] and health insurance.[8] For those individuals receiving government benefits such as public health services, disability benefits, and subsidized housing, this discrimination makes it difficult for individuals to exit the system of government services, at enormous cost to everyone.

In addition, individuals often don't seek treatment because of the stigma associated with it, allowing their illness to escalate both in severity and cost of treatment.[9]

The Media

No policy should be initiated, no process should be planned, and no mental health story should be covered by the media, without direct consultation with people who have experienced the mental health system firsthand.
—Sally Zinman[10]

According to a Massachusetts Association for Mental Health survey, only 10 percent of people surveyed said they obtained information about mental illness from physicians; 27 percent of the respondents cited newspapers and magazines as information sources; and 22 percent named television as their source of information. Unfortunately, mistruths about mental illness often are perpetuated by all of these media.

Everything you read in the newspaper is absolutely true. Except for the rare story of which you happen to have firsthand knowledge.—Erwin Knoll

Although there are excellent articles on mental illness, they don't generally make for such eye-catching headlines as "Mental patient freed to kill,"[11] or lead copy such as "Russell Eugene Weston Jr. told a court-appointed psychiatrist that he stormed the U.S. Capitol last summer, killing two police officers, to prevent the United States from being annihilated by disease and legions of cannibals."[12]

Hollywood movie treatment of mental illness is even more insidious. According to psychiatrist Cleo Van Velsen, who has made a study of Hollywood's treatment of mental illness over the past six decades, mentally ill people "are often wrongly portrayed as violent and that perpetuates the myths about all or the majority of patients being violent. In 'The Silence of the Lambs,' for example, we have the portrayal of an unstable man who is extremely violent. In 'Psycho' you have the sense of violence and the secret basement world, and generally odd people. There is also the danger and violence in 'Halloween' where the man escapes from an asylum. 'Final Analysis' with Richard Gere is another bad example, and so too is 'Copycat' where the patient becomes obsessed with the forensic psychiatrist and tries to kill her."

Dr. Van Velsen notes that movies also trivialize mental illness: "In a lot of the films there is the underlying message that all the patient really needs is love and affection. There is a tendency in films to try and normalize mental illness by saying that patients don't need treatment, they need love. The audience gets the two extremes and what we are not getting are portrayals of people with chronic illness."[13]

Defeating Stigma by First Defeating Inner Stigma

People with mental illness may have to recover from the stigma they have incorporated into their very being.
—William Anthony, Ph.D.[14]

Something we were withholding made us weak until we found it was ourselves. —Robert Frost

There is a great deal of talk about stigma, meaning the negative judgments and discrimination by others, but a far more powerful, damaging stigma is inner stigma. In my own instance, I'd never experienced anything as terrifying as my mind failing me. I'd never even considered that it could. But once it had, I shakily looked for signs everywhere that it might be happening again.

The Wisconsin Blue Ribbon Commission on Mental Health reports:

> Consumers describe self-stigma as a self-fulfilling prophecy that starts when they first receive a diagnosis of mental disorder. Over time, consumers begin internalizing expectations of not making progress or not achieving the same things in life as their peers. The process of internalizing stigma and discrimination is similar to what other devalued groups experience and is magnified by consumer incomes that are often below poverty level. The experience of poverty magnifies the experience of self-stigma. People lose their sense of self-worth, their confidence, and their ability to hope or dream of a better future. Consumers describe this process as 'spirit breaking.' Self-stigma influences people's ability to feel motivated or self-confident and it greatly impedes recovery. The downward spiral of self-worth is further enforced by mental health providers' low expectations and the outside world's stigma and discrimination.[15]

People diagnosed with mental illness often come to see themselves as damaged merchandise—not as strong, or deserving, or likely to succeed as others. Inner stigma is prevalent and harmful and numbing. External stigma might affect whether you get a specific job, apartment or date, but internal stigma affects whether you seek *any* job, apartment, or date.

Individuals can significantly move toward procovery by addressing inner stigma *first*. It is often easier to have an impact on yourself than on others, and helping yourself strengthens you to impact others.

A hospital nurse once said to me, "Kathleen, if you and your daughters were lost in the woods, no food, by your-selves—and you were all hungry, but you only had a tiny bit of food left, what would you do with it?" "Divide it between my daughters," I answered, wondering why people ask such ridiculous questions. "Wrong answer," he said matter of factly. "You should eat it. Because without you they wouldn't have a prayer. You'd need to conserve your strength so that you could care for them. Protecting your-self would be their protection."[16]

Positively affecting your own inner stigma will have last-ing repercussions in your interactions with others.

Get in touch with your deepest feelings about mental ill-ness and you. Deep down, do you harbor any feelings that are less reality than myth? Do you *know* that mental ill-ness is an illness and not a choice? That you are not lazy or weak, that living with mental illness can be the hardest of work? That you are not your diagnosis? That you have enormous potential and worth?

Changing Minds

Revolutions begin when people who are defined as problems achieve the power to redefine the problem.
—John McKnight

If you win your own battle with inner stigma, you will be better equipped to win the battle against outer stigma.

Changing others' minds requires more than disseminating accurate information to contradict the myths; it also requires *positive direct contact*. Information may superficially dispel the myths and lead to politically correct language; but positive personal contact is necessary to complete the job, to affect subconsciously held prejudices.

A great many people think they are thinking, when they are merely rearranging their prejudices.—William James

Erich Fromm, speaking about the nature of reform, states, "The true criterion of reform is . . . the question of whether it goes to the roots and attempts to change causes—or whether it remains on the surface and attempts to deal only with symptoms."[17]

Positive direct contact with individuals diagnosed with

mental illness can get to the roots and provide this realism. This type of contact comes about when people meet on a common level—as colleagues, friends, or neighbors, for example—or for a common goal or organization, such as work, church, a volunteer organization, or a social gathering. These types of connections can help others personally and directly understand that mental illness is just one small fact among the thousands or millions that make up an individual.

A powerful reduction in stigma can be effected from individual to individual.

A new public opinion must be created privately and unobtrusively. The existing one is maintained by the press, by propaganda, by organization, and by financial and other influences which are at its disposal. This unnatural way of spreading ideas must be opposed by the natural one, which goes from man to man and relies solely on the truth of our thoughts and the hearer's receptiveness for new truth. —Albert Schweitzer

Eliminating prejudice is not about thinking we are all the same. It is about recognizing that although we are not all the same, we are all equal, and there is beauty in our differences.

To Speak Out or Not?

An additional question arises when consumers interact with people who are not aware of the consumer's diagnosis. Writing about this issue with regard to stigmatized persons in general, sociologist Erving Goffman states, "The issue is not that of managing tension generated during social contacts, but rather that of managing information about his 'failing.' To display or not to display; to tell or not to tell; to let on or not to let on; to lie or not to lie; and in each case, to whom, how, when, and where."[18]

This question is not about the type of disclosure made to a therapist or confidant or small confidential group, but rather to the wide variety of third parties with whom we have no special relationship yet—perhaps co-workers, fellow church members, neighbors, or a public group.

Goffman discusses in particular the consumer's dilemma if he does not tell: "For example, while the mental patient is in the hospital, and when he is with adult members of his own family, he is faced with being treated tactfully as if he were sane when there is known to be some doubt, even though he may not have any; or he is treated as insane, when he knows this is not just. But for the ex-mental patient the problem can be quite different; it is not that he must face prejudice against himself, but rather that he must face unwitting acceptance of himself by individuals who are prejudiced against persons of the kind he can be revealed to be. Wherever he goes his behavior will falsely confirm for the other that they are in the company of what in effect they demand but may discover they haven't obtained, namely, a mentally untainted person like themselves."[19]

There is a widespread belief that a healing benefit automatically accompanies speaking out. Some would argue that consumers should always speak out and, by doing so, they will reduce external stigma, increase self-efficacy and most important, decrease self-stigma.

Others may find their path to procovery by getting as far away from the mental health system and surrounding issues as possible.

Key in this highly individual decision is that *your choice whether to speak out should not be dependent on how you hope others will accept and respond to your message.* Even given the worst-case scenario of people's responses, some individuals would still opt to speak out, feeling perhaps that disclosure will decrease the feeling of pressure or secrecy, or make it easier to interact with others, or facilitate a sense of pride. If you are such an individual, *regardless of how others react*, speaking out will be better for you. But for individuals who are banking on the supportive reactions of others (and keep in mind that this is with regard to broadly speaking out, not selective disclosure), reactions that they have no control over, there is significant risk of initiating a spiral of diminishing self-esteem.

Consumers who choose not to speak out can provide a different but also effective avenue to reducing stigma. When, after months or years of "regular" contact, others incidentally find out about a consumer's past or present mental disorder, they are shocked that the consumer seems so "normal."

Example is not the main thing in influencing others. It is the only thing. —Albert Schweitzer

This is not in any way to diminish the importance and courage of those who do speak out. This is to say that *not* speaking out can also result in stigma reduction—both internal and external.

Information and contact are both needed to dissolve stigma. But just as there is no single path to procovery, there is no single path to dissolving stigma, and all must be supported and respected.

This world and yonder world are incessantly giving birth: every cause is a mother, its effect the child.

When the effect is born, it too becomes a cause and gives birth to wondrous effects.

These causes are generation on generation, but it needs a very well lighted eye to see the links in their chain.

—Rumi

Procovery Notes for Consumers

❖ **Learn the facts about mental illness**, including that mental illness is an illness and not a personal flaw. Increasing your understanding of mental illness should increase your respect for yourself; in fact, you should be in awe of yourself and your strength and courage in living with mental illness.

❖ **Dispel internal myths**. Although it is inevitable that we absorb some of society's prejudiced and unfounded feelings about mental illness, it is critical on an individual level to examine closely these thoughts and feelings. Are you embarrassed by your diagnosis? Do you feel that you have less potential than you did before your diagnosis? Do you feel your diagnosis is a result of some flaw or weakness in you? Internal stigma reduction can be the best path to external stigma reduction.

Self-esteem is the reputation we acquire with ourselves.
—Nathaniel Branden

❖ **Consider whether the conditions are right for you before speaking out about mental illness.** Will you feel better for speaking out, regardless of how others react?

❖ **When getting to know someone, consider building on areas of commonality before sharing differences.**

Sometimes it helps to develop or remind yourself of everyday things you enjoy discussing—sports, music, movies, books, items in the news—to lead off with in a new relationship. Then when you decide to share other aspects of yourself and your life, you have built some foundation on which to do it. In other words, for some, discussing their illness before developing common ground amounts to wearing their heart on their sleeve.

To wear your heart on your sleeve isn't a very good plan; you should wear it inside, where it functions best. —Margaret Thatcher

❖ **Don't further stigmatize yourself by holding low expectations.** Clearly you need to take care of yourself, operating within healthy individual boundaries. But individuals with chronic mental illness can and do procover, and lead joy-filled lives. Expect that you will do so, too.

❖ **Don't stigmatize yourself by attributing all disappointments to your diagnosis.** People frequently suffer disappointments, setbacks, and feelings of personal failure. Sometimes, when diagnosed with a chronic illness, we attribute more to a diagnosis than we should.

We should be careful to get out of an experience only the wisdom that is in it and stop there; lest we be like

the cat that sits down on a hot stove lid. She will never sit down on a hot stove lid again and that is well; but also she will never sit down on a cold one any more.
—Mark Twain

◈ **Kick at the barriers you encounter in your path to procovery.** It is tough to do, but try not to let stigma knock you off that path. If the first, second, or 20th employer says no; if the first, second, or 20th landlord won't rent to you; if the first, second, or 20th person says no to a date with you, don't let their prejudice affect your ultimate progress along your desired path.

◈ **Take the high road.** Use your anger regarding stigma as fuel to put your life together.

The best revenge is living well. —The Talmud

◈ **Let others get to know you.** Whether others know of your diagnosis up front or learn about it down the road, people out and about are the best means by which to dispel the myths about chronic mental illness. Through working, attending school, or volunteering, your letting others get to know you will help them to see past the label of mental illness to you as a person. Volunteering, although it can be done individually, can also be rewarding as part of a group.

Your [consumer] group should volunteer its services in the community in some substantive way. For example, you can volunteer in hospitals, or public park clean-up units, or to collect and sort trash for recycling, or to visit shut-ins, or read to the blind, or in any number of worthwhile efforts. And when you make it known that you are a group of mental health consumers—mental patients—who are performing this service, and people get to know you as good citizens of their community, this goes a long way toward fighting stigma.
—Susan Rogers[20]

◈ **Let others know how you view their depictions of mental illness—good or bad**. This can be done through phone calls, letters to the editor, etc., individually or as a group.

When your group identifies particularly horrible examples of stigmatizing, sensationalized coverage of mental health issues, or particularly good coverage, you can condemn or congratulate the perpetrators, appropriately. For example, the Mental Health Association of Southeastern Pennsylvania called attention to the issue of stigma by issuing Pie-in-the-Face and Pie-a-la-Mode awards. (Pie was actually an acronym, PI&E, for Public Information & Education.) PI&E-a-la-mode recipients (good guys) received a framed citation and an apple pie; PI&E-in-the-face recipients (bad guys) got a framed citation and a lemon meringue pie, with instructions on applying.

Your group can issue such awards, then do a press release, which will kill two birds with one stone: You will make the point that the media should not stigmatize people diagnosed mentally ill, and may get some positive publicity for your group. —Susan Rogers[21]

❖ **Demand change; exercise your right to a voice.** Policies that perpetuate stigma—from poorer health insurance coverage of mental illness than physical illness to limited funding for research into the causes and treatments of mental illness to inadequate budgets for public mental health services—can be changed if enough people let their representatives know that they want such change.[22] Seek to participate in local health committees and boards. In particular, be ready to answer the specific question, "What do you want?"

❖ **Vote.**

Bad officials are the ones elected by good citizens who do not vote. —George Jean Nathan

Procovery Notes for Family Members

❖ **Listen and validate.** Particularly in view of the lessening availability of therapy, it can be a huge gift to listen and counter self-stigma. Helping individuals re-label their feelings—e.g., not paranoid, not a loser, but instead anxious, or concerned, or nervous—can be a gift. Self-talk can be powerful and generate illness, or generate health. Help generate health.

❖ **Open, don't close dialog**. We need more direct, heartfelt conversations about mental illness. In order to hold these conversations and to dispel myths, we need to allow others to voice their concerns—at least initially—in sometimes awkward, offensive ways. If instead we cut them off at the first moment we take offense, we are likely to change words, but not thinking. Stigma-reducing conversations ultimately lead to understanding, not embarrassment. If you allow people enough room to discuss their views freely, they might get in touch with their prejudice—a necessary step to stigma reduction.

I have learned silence from the talkative, tolerance from the intolerant, and kindness from the unkind; yet strange, I am ungrateful to these teachers.
—Kahlil Gibran

❖ **Don't feel embarrassed or ashamed of things that are a part of everyday life**. Illness, of all types and sizes, *is* a part of everyday life. Your acceptance of this fact, and refusal to feel ashamed or embarrassed, will positively affect others.

Nobody's family can hang out the sign, 'Nothing is the matter here.'—Chinese proverb

❖ **Learn the facts about mental illness**, including that it is an illness and not a personal flaw. Increasing your understanding of mental illness should increase not only the information you have for others but also your respect for the extraordinary courage and strength of both your relative and yourself in the face of adversity.

Acknowledge the remarkable courage your family member may show dealing with a mental disorder.
—Rex Sibling, NAMI Sibling and Adult Children Network[23]

❖ **Demand change from elected officials**. And vote. See the Consumer Procovery Note, above.

❖ **When you are confronted with negativity regarding mental illness**, consider responding in a positive way. Note the contributions of some of the well-known individuals throughout history who have been diagnosed with mental illness,[24] the increasing success at treatment, the increasing number of those who procover and lead productive and fulfilling lives. Try countering a negative observation with, "That has not been my experience . . . "

Studies have shown that the way to counter negative stereotypes is not to discuss them but to replace them with positive images. —Susan Rogers[25]

❖ **Let others know how you view their depiction of mental illness—good or bad.** This can be done through phone calls, letters to the editor, etc., individually or as a group. See the quote by Susan Rogers in Procovery Notes for Consumers, above.

Procovery Notes for Staff

❖ **Examine your own feelings surrounding mental illness**. Although it is inevitable that we absorb some of society's prejudiced and unfounded feelings about mental illness, it is critical on an individual level to examine these thoughts and feelings closely. Do you feel individuals diagnosed with mental illness have less potential than others? That they are personally flawed? That their non-compliance is something other than learning to live with a hellish illness?

❖ **Counter the images presented by the media** not only by dispensing accurate information but also by dispelling the prevalent misinformation about mental illness, as a standard practice to consumers and family members.

❖ **Don't attribute more to the diagnosis than is warranted**. Consumers experience enough stigma outside the office. Don't further stigmatize consumers by invalidating and disrespecting their perceptions and judgments about their illness, including side effects.

❖ **Stand up proud with others**. Staff know well that they themselves are not immune from the stigma attached to mental illness.

'But you're so good! Why would you want to work with chronic schizophrenics? Why waste your talents on

them?' My colleagues are for the most part nice, intelligent people who are devoted to righting society's wrongs and rooting out social injustice whenever and wherever they can; they recycle, wear fake furs, avoid red meat, and give money to the homeless. Nevertheless, they take a dim view of work with chronic mental patients and seem unable to understand why I would choose to do it. —Ann Braden Johnson[26]

Your reply can make the difference not only as to how the other person views mental illness but even more importantly as to how *you* feel. Share why you entered the field, the progress you've seen in treating mental illness. And most important, express how it feels to be a part of someone's procovery.

The truth is, I didn't choose the work; it chose me. Chronically mentally ill people have showed me things I never would have known; they have told me things most people never hear; and they continually amaze me with their generosity and kindness toward each other and to an outside world that treats them like lepers. They have forced me to acknowledge parts of myself I'd rather not even look at, and I am deeply grateful. They have given me so much over the years that I want to do anything I can to pay them back by showing others what I have learned.
—Ann Braden Johnson[27]

1. Anthony, W.A. (1993). "Recovery from mental illness: The guiding vision of the mental health service system in the 1990s." *Psychosocial Rehabilitation Journal*, 16, p. 19.

2. Styron, William (1990). *Darkness Visible: A Memoir of Madness.* New York: Random House, 67-68.

3. According to a 1997 Massachussetts Association for Mental Health survey, more than 40 percent of those surveyed said that they believe most mental illnesses are the result of character flaws and personality defects. "Survey Finds Stigma, Error Haunt Mental Illness," *Boston Globe*, Oct. 3, 1997.

4. The magnitude of the violence risk associated with mental illness is comparable to that associated with age, educational attainment, and gender and is limited to only some disorders and symptom constellations. Barchas, J., M.D. (1998). "New evidence on the violence risk posed by people with mental illness," *Archives of General Psychiatry*, May 1998. Available at www.ama-assn.org/sci-pubs/journals/archive/psyc/vol_55/no_5/ycm8065x.htm or if link is unavailable, home page http://www.ama-assn.org/public/journals/psyc/psychome.htm. See also Monahan, J. (1992). "Mental disorder and violent behavior: attitudes and evidence," *American Psychology*, 1992;47:511-521. Also see Link, B., Stueve, A. (1995). "Evidence bearing on mental illness as a possible cause of violent behavior," *Epidemiol Review*, 1995;17:172-180. Both cited in Link, B. (1998). "New evidence on the violence risk posed by people with mental illness," *General Psychiatry*, 1998; 55 No. 5 (May 1998).

5. Unfortunately, it is our nature to fear that which we don't understand. "Sometimes mentally ill people, when they are very sick, are incomprehensible—that scares people," says Dr. Paul Fink, a past president of the American Psychiatric Association. (Fall 1996 issue of *Treatment Today*). See Fink, Paul and Tasman, A. (1992). *Stigma and mental illness*, Washington, D.C.: American Psychiatric Press.

6. "Study of Mentally Ill Proposed," Associated Press, June 6, 1999.

7. The loss of workplace privacy is a major concern. David F. Linowes, a University of Illinois public policy professor who has been studying workplace privacy since the early 1970s, says that in his 1996 survey of Fortune 500 companies, a third of the 84 respondents said they used medical records to make employment-related decisions. (Source: *Washington Post*, Feb. 8, 1998) In Philadelphia, supervisors at the Southeastern Pennsylvania Transit Authority paid Rite Aid Pharmacy to supply medications to its workers in exchange for a breakdown on who was using what drugs. (Source: *Washington Post*, Feb. 8, 1998)

8. Source: National Alliance for the Mentally Ill. "According to the National Institute of Mental Health, 'Estimates based on studies of current coverage and utilization suggest for an additional annual cost of $6.5 billion . . . annual savings in indirect costs and

general medical services would amount to $8.7 billion. This . . . would represent an estimated net economic benefit for the nation of $2.2 billion annually."

9. Even people who know someone with mental illness, or who have themselves been diagnosed with it, often consider the condition shameful, hindering access to treatment. Massachusetts Mental Health Association survey, cited in "Survey Finds Stigma, Error Haunt Mental Illness," *Boston Globe*, Oct. 3, 1997.

10. Zinman, Sally (1999). "Treatment by Force is an Attack on Rights," *San Jose Mercury News*, June 20, 1999, Section C.

11. *The Guardian*, London, July 22, 1998.

12. *The New Orleans Times-Picayune*, Apr. 25, 1999 (by-line Bill Miller, *Washington Post*).

13. Dobson, Roger (1998). "The bad, sad and crazy movies that mock mental illness." *The Independent—London*, Oct. 10, 1998, p. 3.

14. Anthony, W.A. (1993). "Recovery from mental illness: The guiding vision of the mental health service system in the 1990s." *Psychosocial Rehabilitation Journal*, 16, p. 15.

15. State of Wisconsin Blue Ribbon Commission on Mental Health Final Report (April 1997), p. 58.

16. Crowley, Kathleen (1995). *The Day Room*, San Francisco: Kennedy Carlisle Publishing Co.

17. Fromm, Erich (1955). *The Sane Society*, New York: Holt, Rinehart and Winston, 273.

18. Goffman, Erving (1963). *Stigma: Notes on the management of spoiled identity*, New York: Simon & Schuster, 41-42. Erving Goffman (1922-1983) was professor of sociology at the University of California at Berkeley and the University of Pennsylvania. This book draws extensively on autobiographies and case studies to analyze the stigmatized person's feelings about himself and his strategies in relationship to "normals."

19. Ibid.

20. Rogers, Susan, *Fighting Stigma*, at www.mhasp.ort/chouse/fighting.html, or contact the National Mental Health Consumers' Self-Help Clearinghouse, 1211 Chestnut Street, Philadelphia, PA 19107, 800-553-4539.

21. *Id.*

22. Sibling, Rex. *60 tips on coping with mental illness in the family*. NAMI Sibling and Adult Children Network.

23. Wahl, Otto, Ph.D., George Mason University. *Ten things you can do to fight stigma*. See http://mason.gmu.edu/~owahl/ACTIONS.HTM.

24. For instance, Abraham Lincoln, Isaac Newton, Leo Tolstoy, John Keats, Winston Churchill, Vivian Leigh, Lionel Aldridge, Beethoven, Michelangelo, Ernest Hemingway. Source: National Alliance for the Mentally Ill, "Helpline Fact Sheet: People with mental illness" (1999), http://www.nami.org/helpline/peoplew.htm.

25. Rogers, Susan, *Fighting Stigma*, at www.mhasp.ort/chouse/fighting.html, or contact the National Mental Health Consumers' Self-Help Clearinghouse, 1211 Chestnut Street, Philadelphia, PA 19107, 800-553-4539

26. Johnson, Ann Braden (1990). *Out of Bedlam: The Truth About Institutionalization*. New York: Basic Books, 1.

27. *Id.*

Using Feelings as Fuel

For persons recovering from mental illness . . . emotions are too quickly and routinely considered a part of the illness rather than a part of the recovery.
—William Anthony, Ph.D.[1]

Your vision will become clear only when you can look into your heart. Who looks outside, dreams; who looks inside, awakens. —Carl Jung

The path to procovery is a highly emotional one. I used to feel a victim of and subject to wildly changing moods, a passenger on a mood roller coaster. It took me years to understand that I could climb into the driver's seat and impact those moods.

It can be enormously difficult to form a collaborative treatment relationship, or to keep up with a job, school or a social life, when you have no idea what your mood will be at any given time and whether it will be debilitating. At their most damaging, feelings can spiral into intense depths, into a pit that can be deep and slippery and dangerous—whether the pit is one of depression, or mania, or apathy, or any other dangerous trap.

To make matters more difficult, individuals with psychiatric disabilities may at times have to contend with the essentially insoluble complexity of deciding whether a state of mind is clinical or "real."

Taking a procovery-oriented approach of moving forward through ordinary and incremental actions, individuals can do much not only to *cope* with feelings but also to use feelings as *fuel* for procovery. This is in no way minimizing the depth or hellishness of these feelings, or suggesting that mastering moods is easy or foolproof. But a proactive approach to dealing with feelings can pay enormous returns.

Any of these approaches can help individuals find their own path to using feelings to aid procovery:

- Treating negative emotions as productive components of the path to procovery

- Waiting out certain feelings

- Utilizing emotional radar

- Converting negative feelings into positive results

- Purposefully generating positive emotions

Treating Negative Emotions as Productive Components of the Path to Procovery

Those who do not know how to weep with their whole heart don't know how to laugh either. —Golda Meir

It is a natural but flawed tendency to assume that all

intense or negative feelings are *symptoms* of illness rather than *consequences* of illness and/or the procovery process. Feelings that are consequences of illness and the procovery process include:

1. Grieving for the loss of life as it was

2. Frustrations and consequences of dealing with chronic illness

3. The emotions of daily life

1. Grieving for the loss of life as it was. Although procovery is about moving forward, part of this process will likely involve grieving for being unable to move backward, unable to attain a prior state of health, unable to return to who we were.

Elisabeth Kübler-Ross has written of the stages of grief related to death.[2] Her description of these stages—denial and isolation, anger, bargaining, depression, acceptance, and hope—has been found to be applicable to dealing with grief from a wide variety of losses, including chronic illness.

These stages as they relate to mental illness can look something like this:

• **Denial and Isolation.** Individuals, when first diagnosed with a serious chronic illness, tend to deny it. "This can't be happening." "This doctor and this diagnosis is wrong." Unconnected to and unaware of others who have procovered, one can feel very alone in this stage.

Denial is a common initial response to loss and can
serve an important purpose in the procovery process.
William Anthony, Ph.D., notes that "at particular points
in one's recovery, denial of information prevents the person from becoming overwhelmed. Information can be
perceived as a bomb or a blanket—harsh and hostile or
warm and welcome. Helpers in the mental health system must allow for this variation in the time frame of
information they are providing—and not routinely and
simply characterize denial as non-functioning."

- **Anger.** Many individuals diagnosed with chronic mental illness are initially consumed by rage (a healthy
reaction, given the information and its impact) over the
substantial loss and necessary changes in their lives.

- **Bargaining.** Here the person makes "deals," usually
secretly and often with a higher power, in the hope that
this curse of chronic illness will go away.

- **Depression.** This emotion occurs as an individual
begins to understand the chronic nature of his or her illness. Few individuals escape this emotion—given the
circumstances, how could they?

- **Acceptance.** At this point the person tends to be neither depressed nor angry about the illness but accepting
of it.

- **Hope.** As Elisabeth Kübler-Ross notes, the above stages
"will last for different periods of time and will replace
each other or exist at times side by side. The one thing

that usually persists through all these stages is hope. . . . All our patients maintained a little bit of it and were nourished by it in especially difficult times."

2. Frustrations and consequences of dealing with chronic illness. A review of a wide range of consumer/ medical literature identifies a complex spectrum of emotions felt by individuals on the path to procovery, including ambivalence, anxiety, confusion, denial, despair, embarrassment, envy, fatigue, fear (including fear of never escaping from pain), frustration, guilt, hysteria, inability to cope, loneliness, need to take action, neglect, numbness, being overwhelmed, resentment, sadness, self-doubt, shock, suspicion/paranoia/distrust, and grieving for the perceived loss of being "normal."

Norman Cousins wrote eloquently on the emotional consequences of illness in *Anatomy of an Illness*:

> I know that during my own illness in 1964, my fellow patients at the hospital would talk about matters they would never discuss with their doctors. The psychology of the seriously ill put barriers between us and those who had the skill and the grace to minister to us.
>
> There was first of all the feeling of helplessness—a serious disease in itself.
>
> There was the subconscious fear of never being able to function normally again—and it produced a wall of separation between us and the world of open movement, open sounds, open expectations.

There was the reluctance to be thought a complainer.

There was the desire not to add to the already great burden of apprehension felt by one's family; this added to the isolation.

There was the conflict between the terror of loneliness and the desire to be left alone.

There was the lack of self-esteem, the subconscious feeling perhaps that our illness was a manifestation of our inadequacy.

There was the fear that decisions were being made behind our backs, that not everything was made known that we wanted to know, yet dreaded knowing.

There was the morbid fear of intrusive technology, fear of being metabolized by a data base, never to regain our faces again. There was resentment of strangers who came at us with needles and vials— some of which put supposedly magic substances in our veins, and others which took more of our blood than we thought we could afford to lose. There was the distress of being wheeled through white corridors to laboratories for all sorts of strange encounters with compact machines and blinking lights and whirling discs.

And there was the utter void created by the longing —ineradicable, unremitting, pervasive—for warmth of human contact.[3]

3. Emotions of daily life. Emotions are often messages from the limitless variety of daily things that we experience, and from natural biological processes, the food we eat, the amount of exercise or sleep we get, the weather, the time of day or month or year, the ripple effect of others.

Treating emotions as a productive part of the path to procovery means working with them as partners, not hiding them as embarrassing skeletons in the closet. Individuals are often told to calm down, to be "rational." This is frequently a misunderstanding of what is rational. Psychoanalyst Erich Fromm writes in *The Art of Listening* that rational behavior is that "which furthers the growth and development of a structure." Many of these emotions can in fact further growth if expressed, or further sickness if suppressed. Releasing them is rational; what is irrational is to bury them.

One needs to ask, what can I learn from this mood? Is it merely a kneejerk or rote response to a situation, a repetition of past emotional habits? Or is it a message about the present—maybe you're being treated disrespectfully, or not getting enough sleep, or rightfully angry, or needing to grieve? Far too often we downplay or discount the feelings that carry important messages for daily life as "just a mood," and in doing so we lose the message by killing the messenger.

Deciding Whether to Work Out or Wait Out a Feeling

Several things help me ride out spells of gloom and depression, keep me from getting trapped in the cycle of despair. One is that since I have been through that tunnel before, I know that there is an end to it and I can go through it. Also, since I more often feel good than bad, I can assume that bad feelings will in time give way to good ones.
—John Holt

The decision of whether to work out or wait out a feeling is complex for those in the process of procovery. If procovery is looking forward, one might ask, then isn't it a contradiction to seek to move toward procovery by reaching back into the past to work through feelings?

Not surprisingly, the answer differs among individuals, and even for the same individual over time. In the case of trauma and/or abuse, for example, it is generally crucial to work through feelings related to these past experiences—both to affect the present and to stop dangerous cycles from perpetuating in the future. Therapy is often a life-saving ingredient, helping one release the past in order to move on to the future.

To really break free of old patterns that no longer serve you, you must first identify where they got their roots, and then pull these roots out and plant new seeds.
—Heather Emelin Graham

The very success of psychopharmacology in treating serious mental illness has had the unfortunate effect of minimizing the importance of psychotherapy in healing patients and keeping them alive.—Kay Redfield Jamison

Deciding how much attention a particular feeling warrants is tricky stuff. Consider:

• Have you had this feeling before? Is the feeling intense or bothersome or reoccurring in the sense that it appears to warrant exploration? Can you identify why you have it?

• How long before this feeling is likely to go away on its own? Will this feeling matter in the long view—one week, one month, or one year from now? For instance, anger due to waiting in a long line at a grocery store will probably be over in a short while regardless of whether one expresses anger, but anger felt as a result of your personal experience of the horror of war is likely to continue to surface and hinder procovery until released in a safe, productive manner.

• Have you accurately assessed a particular situation? Imagine feeling brushed off at a party and assuming the person doesn't like you, when in reality that person felt an immediate but painful attraction to you, as you reminded him or her of a much-loved sibling who recently died. Or suppose several times you attempt to initiate a conversation with someone, and the person doesn't respond. You feel this is a reflection on you when in fact that person has a hearing disability and simply did not hear you. Sometimes it pays to reconsider whether your take on a particular situation is accurate.

Developing Emotional Radar

Over the years, my parishioners have taught me two lessons. When cast into the depths, to survive we must first let go of things that will not save us. Then we must reach out for things that can. —Forrest Church

My husband can watch the same movie 10 times and, each time, even years later, like a reflex, will laugh at the same places. Unlike much of illness and life, where each day might bring a new and unique challenge, feelings can often be Pavlovian responses that repeat themselves.

Because of this, an individual's life experience can help him or her to "develop radar," to head unwanted feelings off at the pass, to recognize ahead of time when a mood is developing that might act as a deterrent to procovery. For example, when frustration will likely turn to anger, or anger to crippling depression.

The very same triggers and boundaries that have one effect for some individuals can have the opposite effect for others. A late night snack might improve the quality of sleep of some individuals, but it might disturb the sleep of others.

By paying attention to this highly personal information about how one's actions affect one's moods, over time individuals can become leading experts on their personal patterns and triggers and boundaries.

Using emotional radar, an individual can develop approaches that prevent or avoid or reduce the impact of repeated negative emotions. Such approaches could include:

- Waiting it out. As noted above, experience will sometimes allow one to know that a feeling will likely give way, and that energy used to dispel it could be put to better use.

- Finding safe, productive ways to express feelings. Safely expressing feelings, even when the underlying facts cannot be changed, can be of significant therapeutic value. (For some ideas, see the Procovery Notes following this chapter.)

  The thing to do with feelings is to make it safe to feel all of them. —Robyn Posin

- Avoidance of making high-level or long-term decisions—such as quitting a job or school, deciding to move, changing a medication—when in low-level or short-term moods.

Emotional radar can further alert us to bring a ladder into the pit if prevention and early intervention efforts haven't worked—the ladder being those steps that have proved in the past to help through crises.

Converting Negative Feelings into Positive Results

Feelings are good servants, still better friends, but terrible masters. —Grow, Inc. Blue Book

Negative feelings need not always begin a spiral downward; sometimes they can be converted into positive results, and even fuel for procovery. Strategies to do this include:

- **Determining, before taking action, if you have accurately labeled the feeling**. People sometimes label their feelings quickly without thinking them through. This is easy to do, as some feelings feel remarkably like other feelings—an individual can initially identify a feeling as being anger and later realize he or she was actually disappointed, or initially identify a feeling as being depression and later realize it was anger, or initially identify a feeling as fear and later realize it was excitement.

   Because feelings can be a map for our actions, using incorrect labels will be like following a map where the street signs are wrong. As Erich Fromm noted in *The Art of Listening*, "As long as you start with the wrong premise, the problem is insoluble."

- **Using feelings as fuel.** As with acute pain, uncomfortable feelings can have a role in procovery in that they can create a compelling reason to act. It is easy to see negative feelings as an indication that one is doing something wrong. In fact, these feelings are often not just a fall-out of illness but precursors to actions leading to procovery.

Loneliness, instead of reinforcing isolation, can be fuel to find ways to meet and connect with others. Guilt, instead of being the knife turned inward, can lead to the productive expression of anger. Frustrations at the inequities of the mental health system, instead of leading to quitting the system entirely, can lead to advocacy. Depression, instead of leading to numbness, can lead to a positive change in medications or doctors or a change in living situation. Feeling consistently overwhelmed or rushed might lead to preparing a little earlier (or committing to simplify or do less) to reduce the pressured feeling.

Purposefully Generating Positive Emotions

You are only one thought away from a good feeling.
—Sheila Krystal.

Negative emotions tend to build on one another. So do positive ones, hence the ripple effect. Additionally, as noted earlier, we tend to develop conditioned responses to things, Pavlovian responses that can be negative or positive.

Consider the preparation that might go into the setting for a romantic evening—candlelight, flowers, music—all things you know you enjoy, all done to create a mood.

Rather than feeling victimized by moods, responding to feelings as they come, it is sometimes possible to create them. Examples are:

- Starting a day by making a list of 10 things that are good in your life, or by singing in the shower or using a scented shower gel, or listening to a motivational tape or uplifting music, or making blueberry pancakes.

- Making a conscious effort to notice which people you consistently feel good around and which people you consistently feel worse around.

- Reorganizing all or part of your living space to your specific liking, affecting a cozy, cluttered look surrounded by things you love; or creating a sparse, simple look, by eliminating "stuff" for the most part; putting a post-it note with the words "Just Start Anywhere" on a mirror; or painting clouds on your ceiling or the word YES! in bright colors.

- Look, too, at what you enjoy, ignoring whether you can justify it or even identify why you like it, or whether you gain anything from it. "I know it's a waste of time, but I just love doing jigsaw puzzles . . . " "I'm taking a belly dancing class, don't ask me when I'll ever get to do it . . . "

Many men go fishing all of their lives without knowing that it is not the fish they are after.
—Henry David Thoreau

Procovery Notes for Consumers

❖ **Sometimes, in an attempt to not feel a feeling, we actually prolong feeling it**. For example, individuals may feel angry but intellectualize their feelings by justifying others' behavior—"He didn't mean to hurt me," or "Oh, she doesn't realize her remark was offensive"—only to find themselves still angry and still justifying the behavior weeks later. Just like you can't leave a place you've never been, some feelings need to be felt before you can let go of them.

At home, I dream that at Naples, at Rome, I can be intoxicated with beauty and lose my sadness. I pack my trunk, embrace my friends, embark on the sea and at last wake up in Naples, and there beside me is the stern fact, the sad self, unrelenting, identical, that I fled from. I seek the Vatican and the palaces. I affect to be intoxicated with sights and suggestions, but I am not intoxicated. My giant goes with me wherever I go.
—Ralph Waldo Emerson

❖ **Finding "safe," productive ways to vent, express, and release can have tremendous positive impact**:

- Vigorous exercise. As Maureen Wixon, M.A. has stated, "Anger is a very physical emotion, and exercise can take the edge off. . . . After a good workout, the intensity of anger can be lessened, allowing men and women the chance to examine the situation in a more coherent way."

- A good cry

- Writing a letter (whether or not you send it) or creating a "self-dialog" by keeping a journal

  Writing free verse is like playing tennis with the net down. —Robert Frost

- A cup of tea with a friend

- A theater group

"What I have found is that my present continues to look like my past when I try to deny or to stifle my feelings or to 'move on' before I am really ready to do so." —Heather Emelin Graham

❖ **Find ways to express yourself which make you feel better in the long run**. Don't just react. For instance, individuals have described abruptly going off their meds, that they felt were greatly helping them, because they felt angry with their doctor and knew of no other way to express their anger. This is a case of cutting off your nose to spite your face.

A life of reaction is a life of slavery, intellectually and spiritually. One must fight for a life of action, not reaction. —Rita Mae Brown

❖ **Difficulty in getting in touch with and reading your own feelings** can come about as a result of many factors, including trauma and/or abuse. Take special care to begin allowing yourself to feel feelings in a safe manner. Perhaps with a trusted support group and/or therapist, or a personal journal, or a close friend.

"When I left the hospital, I was not entirely "cured" of my eating disorder, but I had been given an invaluable gift: the beginnings of self-respect. It was also the beginning of being able to question the veracity of my beliefs about myself and about my life—of seeing that my eating disorder might not be all that was eating me, but instead might be only the symptom of much deeper issues. I began to climb out of the little box I had been living inside and to start to recognize and acknowledge the impact of my past upon my life and to experience for the first time the feelings I had locked away deep inside me." —Heather Emelin Graham

❖ **If something won't matter in the long term**, it might not be worth getting worked up about in the short term, either.

The art of being wise is the art of knowing what to overlook. —William James

❖ **Avoid making high-level or long-term decisions when in low-level or short-term moods.** The times we most want to act are often when moods are most intense. This can be the least effective time to analyze options and to take action.

❖ **Take the long view also with respect to your responses to your feelings.** Someone with diabetes may find his taste buds screaming for a forbidden snack. Someone on her way to overcoming substance abuse may often feel that every part of her being is calling for a drink. But the loudest feeling isn't necessarily the one that will get you where you want to go in the long run.

❖ **Don't buy into a cycle of despair.** Remind yourself that a sudden change of feeling may be inside you, and not a reflection of the outside world.

On those days when life seems without hope and I feel that man and his works are doomed, I try to remind myself that this doom is in me, not out there. This does not make the gloom go away, or even stop the world from looking hopeless. But I do not get trapped in a cycle of despair—I feel bad, so the world looks bad, so I feel worse, so it looks worse, and so on. —John Holt

❖ **Create moods.** Start your own running list of mood enhancers. Specific books, movies, music, people, places, hobbies. Or specific actions, such as exercising, straightening up your place, wearing something special, helping someone else.

What is changed by my feelings is not what is out there but what I think I and others may be able to do about them. —John Holt

✥ **If you've decided a particular mood has nothing for you to gain from it**, rather than trying to get away from it, perhaps by pouring a drink or climbing into bed, try heading for a positive feeling instead by doing something you love, like playing guitar, roller skating, or shooting hoops.

✥ **Overcome unpleasant feelings about the past** by correcting for someone else what wasn't done for you. For instance, if you experience depression around the holidays each year, due to unhappy childhood memories of this time, consider volunteering to help create a wonderful holiday for children at a local mission.

✥ **Stoke your endorphins**. Laugh.

I love laughing. —William Blake

✥ **Some days are to be lived without attaching any extraordinary meaning to the day**. Sometimes, it can be enough just to make it through the day, the hour, or the next five minutes. Expecting more than this from yourself at times can actually impede your procovery.

✥ **Become aware of who in your life might serve as a grounding person** when your feelings become intense. Also become aware of who might affect you in the opposite way—who pushes your buttons.

◈ **Create a "ladder for the pit,"** a prevention plan so that when you know you're falling you have ideas how to get out. Make a list when you are stable for when you are not and put it (perhaps multiple copies) somewhere handy. The list might include music to play/ music not to; things to do/things not to do; whom to call/whom not to.

◈ **In your prevention plan perhaps include "code words"** so that if you are not feeling verbal you can still easily get your needs across. For example, "I feel dark" might indicate you'd benefit from an increase in lighting or specific music or getting out and around others. "I feel scared" might indicate that a hug, assurance, or company would help. "I feel angry" might mean a need to vent or have company for a jog.

◈ **Fake it 'til you make it**. Like dressing for the job you want rather than the job you have, pretending you are feeling the way you want to feel can move you in that direction. (Note: This is not intended in any way to suggest that "faking it" is an effective long-term strategy. Many people, particularly abuse victims, have had to "fake it" through much of their lives, and only after great struggle have successfully brought their feelings to the fore.)

◈ **Examine your inner dialog, those running messages you send yourself**. Talk to yourself differently, the way you might a close friend—lovingly, supportively. Just like some people save their best dishes for company, some treat a friend in a similar situation much kinder than they do themselves. We often say negative things to ourselves throughout the day that we would *never* allow others to say to us.

◈ **Prepare more; do less**. The natural reaction to feeling good can be to want to "catch up" from feeling bad. This can mean filling days with too much, thus creating an overwhelming and counterproductive feeling of being pressured. Making fewer commitments, leaving for appointments earlier than necessary, and allowing windows of time without any commitments can prevent a slew of negative emotions, including feeling rushed and pressured.

Procovery Notes for Family

◈ **Listen**. Particularly with the lessening availability of therapy, being a gentle listener can be of enormous benefit. Recognize that what may seem like an emotional overreaction may instead be a rational reaction to an overwhelming set of circumstances and resulting emotions. Productive venting of what seems like irrational feelings can lead to rational action.

When we honestly ask ourselves which persons in our lives mean the most to us, we often find that it is those who, instead of giving much advice, solutions, or cures, have chosen rather to share our pain and touch our wounds with a gentle and tender hand. The friend who can be silent with us in a moment of despair or confusion, who can stay with us in an hour of grief and bereavement, who can tolerate not-knowing, not-curing, not-healing and face with us the reality of our powerlessness, that is the friend who cares.

—Henri J. M. Nouwen

❖ **For some individuals, anger is like a bucket** and once emptied they are lighter and freer and healthier. It's easy to downplay, be annoyed, or hurt by anger expressed over something that happened years ago. But often allowing the expression of bottled-up anger, no matter how seemingly trivial or terrifyingly huge, can be a release in itself, and the anger will finally begin to dissipate. In addition to or instead of you being the listener, explore alternative, productive venting arrangements, such as a support group, journaling, therapy or the other ideas in the Procovery Notes for Consumers, above.

To express anger honestly, to express feelings honestly—to describe what we see, or what we have observed, or what we think has happened—and to describe how we feel about it—clears the air, opens the door to productive communication.

—Nathaniel Branden

❖ **For other individuals (or sometimes for the same
individual at a different time), anger builds
upon itself**, and the more expressed the more it is
felt. If you sense this is the case, remember that you
are not and need not be a punching bag—and allowing
yourself to be one is not in the interest of your loved
one's procovery.

❖ **The path to procovery is likely to be very trying
for all concerned**. The same seemingly innocent
question, such as, "Have your side effects subsided at
all?" that can one day elicit a tender response of grati-
tude for your interest, can another day bring a sarcas-
tic, "Thanks for bringing it up—I was just forgetting
all that for a while." Agreeing on expressions, such as
"Today is a good day" or "I'm having a hard day"—or
"I feel like talking today" or "I feel quiet today"—can
pave the way for conversations where desired and cut
known irritants off at the pass.

❖ **Try to maintain perspective, and to avoid the
cycle of negative emotional contagion**. If your
loved one is having a hellish day, it can help to
empathize with him or her regarding the difficulty
of the present, but still maintain perspective and
a hopeful attitude toward the future.

Procovery Notes for Staff

❖ **Listen and accept feelings.** Listening can offer a tremendous release. Listening can allow an individual to blow off enough steam so that he or she can begin to consider options effectively.

❖ **Validate.** As in, "Of course you're furious," "I'm sorry your feelings are hurt," "I can see why you are excited." Validating feelings doesn't mean agreeing with them; it might mean extending the benefit of the doubt, not judging the "appropriateness" of a specific feeling.

For instance, even if you *know* that an individual is misperceiving events, responding to the facts instead of validating the feelings can miss an important opportunity—the opportunity to together develop a clearer understand of what is at the core of these feelings.

It is tempting to believe that this type of validation is inapplicable to individuals experiencing psychotic or delusional episodes. The risks, however, are that 1) it is possible to over-diagnose emotions of individuals with psychiatric disorders as psychotic or delusional, and 2) any invalidation has a treatment cost directly proportional to the loss of trust and self-efficacy. Middle grounds are worth exploring.

One psychiatrist repeatedly attempted to discuss medications with a consumer who refused, and insisted on discussing the radio waves from City Hall that he felt were interfering with his brain waves. The psychiatrist's solution was to compromise by agreeing with the consumer to discuss *neither* medications nor the City Hall radio waves, which ended a stalemate and opened the door to a dialog.

◈ **Many individuals (including many victims of trauma and/or abuse) learn as a survival instinct to numb over.** Their feelings become their enemy, and after time are too buried and complex to get in touch with. Skills that need to be learned may include: getting in touch with feelings, building trust, developing a sense of entitlement, developing feelings of self-esteem and self-efficacy, assertiveness, and expressing anger. Even if therapy is not available for these individuals, staff can make a major difference through their daily interactions by keeping these difficulties in mind, and slowly helping build trust, collaboration, and self-efficacy in their treating relationship.

◈ **Pay attention to specific triggers and patterns, both positive and negative.** Together create a plan for when moods spiral, including words to use. Put the domino effect to positive use.

◈ **Together explore ways to accurately relabel feelings.** "I'm exhausted," instead of, "I'm so lazy." "I am lonely," instead of, "No one likes me." "I feel confused," instead of, "I'm so stupid."

❖ **Together explore ways to convert feelings into action**. "I'm exhausted" into a change in sleeping patterns, or medication timing. "I'm lonely" into, "Here is how I might connect with people." "People are always taking advantage of me," into, "Here is a step I can take to begin the process of being more assertive."

❖ **Agreeing on expressions or "code words" that communicate what you need to know can facilitate communication and reduce irritants**. (See the Procovery Note for Consumers, above, that discusses code words.)

❖ **Keep in mind that many emotions will be experienced in the process of procovery** and respect them as part of the path to healing, rather than automatically relegating them to the category of illness.

❖ **Remember the power of "together" and "we."**

---

1. Anthony, W.A. (1993). "Recovery From Mental Illness: The Guiding Vision of the Mental Health Service System in the 1990s," *Psychosocial Rehabilitation Journal*, 16, p. 11-23.

2. Kübler-Ross, Elisabeth (1969). *On Death and Dying*, New York: Macmillan Publishing Company.

3. Cousins, Norman (1979). *Anatomy of an Illness*, New York:Bantam Books, p. 153.

Gathering Support

Independence? That's middle-class blasphemy. We are all dependent on one another, every soul of us on earth.
—George Bernard Shaw

Well we all need someone we can lean on. And if you want it, well you can lean on me.
—Mick Jagger and Keith Richards

Individuals heal not only holistically but ecologically, not only personally but in the context of their environment.

It was because of the support of others that I procovered. People need people, plain and simple.

It is both a healing strategy and an objective in itself for individuals to be able to form the relationships they seek with others—service providers, colleagues, family, friends, or lovers—in a manner that promotes and maintains their procovery.

The ideas and strategies in this chapter, as within this book, are not specific measures of success or rigid definitions of healing, but rather constitute a toolbox of possible choices that can be used to develop personalized approaches for different individuals.

Match the Supporter to the Support

You will always find some Eskimos ready to instruct the Congolese on how to cope with heat waves.—Stanislaw Lec

Once you receive a diagnosis of chronic illness, you might feel as though there is no one to turn to immediately for support, and the fear of going it alone can be terrifying. And even people blessed with others to turn to from the beginning often live in constant fear that their support will burn out and bail out, tired of dealing with the day-to-day issues of chronic illness.

Adding to this vulnerability and fear of going it alone, individuals often do not consider sources of support outside of the circle of those to whom they are closest. Unfortunately, this decreases the likelihood that all of one's support needs will be met effectively. Looking to someone for support because you need it and because he or she loves you leaves out crucial variables in the support equation.

First, we all have different skill sets, experiences, strengths, and weaknesses. Some of us are more "touchy-feely," comfortable and in tune with our own feelings and those of others. Others would be happy to repair a leaky faucet, balance our checkbook, or paint our entire home but would freeze at the slightest mention of emotions. Some are extraordinary at working with health care issues; others are passive and uncomfortable at doing so. And in general, we cannot do for others what we cannot do for ourselves.

Second, those who love us may be unable or unwilling because of financial, time, or other constraints of everyday life to provide all of the support needed.

On the other side, people often want to help but don't know how. Or they would be happy to lend a hand but it would not occur to them to offer.

Rather than looking for one person to do ten things, it can make an enormous difference to spread support needs around and match the support to the supporters, considering their strengths (and, over time, their history with you) and your current needs. Depending on the type of support that is most important to you at the time, here are questions to help you think about where someone might help:

Grounding: When your mood begins to overtake you, does someone in particular have the ability to bring you back, perhaps just with the sound of his or her voice? Who makes you feel safe? Who strikes you as particularly stable and makes *you* feel that way?

Enticing to move forward: Who can entice you to get out of bed or off the couch when needed? Who can talk you into focusing more on life and less on illness when asked? Not prodding or nagging, as in, "You really need to get out of bed" (unless that's what works for you), but rather inviting, as in, "There are some fresh blueberries and cream on the table if you're interested!"

Build-up: Who can build you up when you're down? Who knows your potential and will remind you of it? Who will remind you of past successes? Who will remind you of what is important in the big picture—*your* big picture?

Daily support: Do you know someone who might be willing to pick something up at the market for you, do a load of laundry, help pay the bills, help you find an apartment, pick up a prescription, or whatever it takes to get through the sometimes overwhelming tasks of daily living?

Listening and/or venting: Who understands you and can offer a shoulder to cry on, be a gentle listener? Who listens in a way that you know you have been heard? Who will allow you to voice your frustration and pain, understanding when you are seeking an outlet and not a solution?

Advice/Problem-solving: Whose judgment do you value on the daily acts of living? Who can you ask, "Do you think I was wrong?" or "Do you think I should ask her out?" or "What do you think I should do?" Is there someone who is proven to understand your particular path and problem-solve or brainstorm or offer advice for you to get there? Someone who seems particularly creative and gifted at finding solutions, someone who easily thinks "out of the box"?

Transportation: Who is willing to help you get where you want to go, including church, work, a dance, or a doctor appointment? Or accompany you on a dry run on public transportation? Or perhaps give you a lift in return for a contribution for gas or parking expenses?

Socializing: Who are you energized by and generally enjoy seeing? Who do you like to go to the movies with or out for lunch with? Who makes you laugh?

Work: Who might help you identify possible job opportunities, craft a resume, practice interviewing, analyze the pros and cons of different opportunities? Help you choose appropriate attire for interviewing and work?

Crisis: Who can help you prevent a personal crisis from turning into a psychiatric crisis? Who understands you, your health issues, the system, etc.? Who is cool under pressure and makes smart decisions that promote procovery as *you* define it?

Shake it up: Who helps you shake it up? Wakes up the courage and desire in you to try new things? Introduces you in a safe, fun way to exciting options available within your community?

Finances: Who can help you with your personal finances? With opening and balancing a checking account, doing tax returns, sorting through benefits? With saving and investing advice?

Organizing and simplifying: Who do you know who is really organized? Who could help you prioritize and simplify? Who might be able to help you structure a personal daily routine (where the goal is to create a life, not a schedule) that takes into account your sometimes overwhelming appointments and commitments, medication timing, and optimum bedtime? Who could help you create a routine that encompasses other important wants and needs such as self-care, socializing, etc.?

By spreading your various support objectives around and by targeting the support to the person, you can both make it easier on your supporters and more likely your needs will be met.

Initially you may not know even one person you feel comfortable turning to for support, and some people may back away when they hear of a psychiatric diagnosis. But over time others will enter your life when you least expect it and—if you let them—will absolutely astonish you with their compassion and generosity.

Approaches to Eight Challenges in Gathering Support for Procovery

When spider webs unite, they can tie up a lion.
—Ethopian proverb

What helps one day can hurt another day. The procovery process is complicated because day-to-day moods change. This is not only because of the complexity and changeability of chronic illness but also because of the natural vacillation between what Norman Cousins described as "the conflict between the terror of loneliness and the desire to be left alone." The same question that will elicit a positive response one day might provoke a very negative one the next. For instance, being asked, "Have you taken your meds?" or, "Can I get you something to eat?" one day might result in you feeling loved or that someone cares. Another day it may result in you feeling angry, feeling, "I'm an adult, don't nag me, let me take care of myself!"

This can be frustrating for all concerned. Communication can aid this problem, perhaps by developing an agreed upon way of letting others know your current mood. "I'm feeling fine right now," might be agreed upon as meaning "I can take care of myself; I'd rather not be pampered." "I'm feeling awful" might mean, "*Anything* you can do or suggest would be appreciated."

Word consciousness. Communication that could lead to increased understanding can be stunted by fears of using the wrong word. Unless you feel someone is trying to be offensive, it can be helpful to try to get past the words in order to facilitate communication and build bridges. Over time, these bridges will enable you to discuss the power of words and their stigmatizing impact—but early on, such a discussion can block communication and suffocate growth.

Burn-out. Many consumers feel that although they have no choice but to live with a psychiatric illness, their loved ones do. Loved ones can leave, and they might. As a result, consumers often live in fear of abandonment, in fear of burning others out, in fear of asking for too much help, of being too dependent. This can lead to a consumer not asking for help needed to prevent a crisis, and ultimately requiring more help because of one. It can be useful for consumers and loved ones to agree that loved ones will take care of themselves first and foremost.

In addition, sometimes people will need to remind themselves and each other that they are on the same team. When life's situations deal stress and difficulty, whether it is being fired from a job or the horrors of war or psychiatric illness, working as a team requires that each member blame the *situation* and not the individuals.

Uncertainty that one is helping. People who are working hard to make a difference like to know they are doing so. And with no tangible indication that they are, they sometimes feel their efforts are in vain. I remember my mother visiting me day after day. I didn't speak to her or often acknowledge her. And yet she visited me on the ward or at home, held my hand and talked to me for hours about her day, about my precious daughters, about some new restaurant she was dying to take me to. How she grounded me—how she impacted my procovery—all without knowing it until years later. The answer to this challenge is to recognize that people working hard to make a difference often *are* making a difference, even if they don't see immediate signs. Faith in the possibility of procovery is self-fulfilling.

Not "feeding into laziness." Mental illness can really

look very self indulgent and lazy to others. And yet, for individuals coping with psychiatric illnesses, there are times that just getting out of bed, showering, dressing can be harder work than the toughest triathlon, than the worst 16-hour job. It can be easy for support persons to confuse their role, to think it is their job to get someone to "buck up," to stop being "lazy." And yet an invitation to life, such as the smell of fresh baked cookies, a CD playing, or a restaurant reservation, can be far more effective in the long run than shaming someone into immediate action.

Matching peer support. Sometimes two individuals both starting the process of procovery find themselves acting as support persons to each other. Although at times this works, as a general practice it may be best to avoid this where possible. It can be complicated when both people face similar crises and dilemmas at the same time and find themselves unable to help each other or themselves.

Seeing the ordinary as extraordinary. It's easy to think big problems demand big solutions. But most of what really matters in life is the ordinary. A touch of the hand, a phone call, a comic strip in the mail, homemade soup, anything that makes someone feel less alone, more visible, more connected.

Viewing personal preferences as symptoms of illness. In gathering support or helping others do so, it is important not to make the mistake of viewing personal preferences as symptoms of illness. For instance, we all have different socialization needs and preferences. And a single individual's needs and preferences will likely vary over time. This can become confusing in that social withdrawal can be a symptom of psychiatric illness or a sign of healing. Some individuals find that social withdrawal to "protect" themselves from other's negative moods is critical at times, or they might find their local support group more disabling than enabling. Or they find an enormous amount of sleep is required to adjust to a new job or a medication change. Or perhaps they are trying to avoid temptations they feel particularly vulnerable to, such as alcohol, gambling, unsafe sex, etc. These real-life factors are essential components of procovery and need to be taken into account before concluding that someone's degree of social contact (or any other personal preference) is a measure of health or illness.

Communicating Effectively

Each relationship you have with another person reflects the relationship you have with yourself. —Alice Deville

Effective communication can be the most simple of concepts and complex of human endeavors. All individuals have much to gain, and much to lose, from the effectiveness of their communications with friends, family, professionals, and others.

Some communication strategies to consider:

Be clear—about what you want and what you don't want.

Be specific rather than general, as in, "I would really like it if we saw a movie Saturday night," rather than, "We never do anything fun together any more."

Don't mind-read. Don't assume you know what the other person is feeling or what he or she *really* means.

Present and resolve only one issue at a time.

Don't continue arguing your points after an issue has been resolved—let it go.

The timing of conversation can have a huge impact on the outcome. Don't choose times when one party is hurried or stressed to discuss important issues. In addition, avoid negative issues at meal times and bed times.

Argue ideas not people. Rather than "You are ridiculous for thinking that . . . ," consider "I disagree with the idea that . . . "

Recognize and set boundaries, and respect the boundaries set by others. Examples: "Please don't call me before 10 a.m. or after 10 p.m."; "I don't want to discuss that right now, maybe we could talk about it this weekend"; "I'd like to attend this doctor appointment with you (or alone)."

Make more "I" statements about your feelings than "you" statements about someone else's feelings, behavior and motivations. Rather than

"You're angry and want to leave me," consider "I feel scared because I think you might leave."

Words Are Not the Only Means of Communication

Sometime we shall have to stop overvaluing the word. We shall learn to realize that it is only one of many bridges that connect the island of our soul with the great continent of common life. —Rainer Maria Rilke

Ah, if you could dance all that you've just said, then I'd understand. —Nikos Kasantakis, Zorba the Greek

Most of what is taught about communicating focuses on the words we use. But some people don't best express themselves through words. And for most individuals diagnosed with psychiatric disorders, there are times when symptoms, moods, or medications will disorder expression and/or make words not easily available.

Unfortunately there is an enormous bias, in most cultures, that assumes that individuals who do not express themselves verbally either are lazy or not very bright or have no preferences about an issue. This bias can have devastating consequences for individuals in medical treatment. When their verbal communications are incapacitated and their non-verbal communications ignored, treatment choices may be made in direct opposition to their needs.

This challenge can run deep for individuals and professionals working through procovery from chronic mental illness. Edward Hall notes, in *Beyond Culture*, that, "Before working with architects, I had been intimately involved with psychiatrists and psychoanalytic schools as well as diplomats. Both are highly verbal and depend for their livelihood and their status on adeptness with spoken words. They can take words, and translate them into ideas and even emotions. One has to use words well if one wants to communicate with either group. Having become habituated to words after working with these two professions, my first contact with architects came as a shock. It was like working with an entirely new tribe about which I knew nothing. I learned that one had to reach this group through their eyes with pictures, not words."

Part of the challenge of aiding procovery is: (1) not to assume that the absence of words is the absence of opinions, preferences, or intentions; and (2) to accept and listen to the wide range of other forms of communications available—from a sigh or a smile, to a tear or a touch, to a prayer or a painting.

As M.C. Richards writes, "I learned through my hands and my eyes and my skin, what I can never learn through my brain."

Socializing *Toward* Procovery

Each friend represents a world in us, a world possibly not born until they arrive, and it is only by this meeting that a new world is born.—Anais Nïn

Many people have a hard time keeping up with their social relations. Complicate the equation with a chronic illness, and socializing can seem ultimately more frustrating than rewarding.

And some individuals grappling with chronic illness tend to "black or white" socializing—moving between avoiding social contact altogether and immersion in the typical bar or noisy, large-crowd party scenes. Neither of these may be moving the individual toward procovery.

What is procovery-oriented socializing? Socializing that furthers growth, that increases one's sense of joy. Something one is happy to have done even if one doesn't "meet" anybody. Something one feels better, not worse, for having done. Compare a hangover after a late-night party with—joining a book or movie club; getting some friends together and swapping skills such as haircuts, manicures, cooking, cleaning, computer skills, guitar lessons; attending or holding a mini-swap meet; exchanging CDs, music, books, videos, and clothes; forming a bulk-buying co-op for health foods; starting a positive club or a procovery club; taking a class; making holiday gifts together; volunteering somewhere.

A variety of strategies can aid procovery-oriented socializing, including:

- If social activity aids your procovery, but the problem is an inability to commit (perhaps due to not knowing how you'll feel at the time, or changing work hours, etc.), try to find "drop-in" or "open" activities.

• If emotional contagion is an issue, in that you are at a shaky stage in your procovery and others' negative moods greatly impact you, you might choose to snuggle up and read inspiring books and watch hopeful movies, rather than running the risk of having your mood drastically affected. During these times, you might limit your social activities to tried and true individuals who always make you feel better for having seen them.

• If you have a friend who you enjoy socializing with, but are not on even grounds with financially—i.e., one of you always treats to movies or expensive restaurants—and the other is in no position to reciprocate, talk openly about your concerns. You might find the person paying views the imbalance in finances as evened out by the balance of companionship. Or you can agree to get together for inexpensive outings such as watching the sunset, taking a walk, volunteering together, or having a potluck.

• Sometimes the fear of prejudice or rejection or loneliness can lead individuals to feel unsafe venturing out of a particular group with which they have grown to identify themselves. In the field of mental health, some individuals isolate themselves, socializing only with others also in this area. If one derives strength and pleasure from doing so, great. But if one feels the world is limited, or shrinking, it pays to find comfortable ways to venture out. Increase your comfort level by branching out with someone you know and are comfortable with, gathering as much information as possible ahead of time about dress, costs, etc. If it is, for example, a gym, a country line-dancing class, or a class at a local college, you might attend on an observation-only or audit basis the first time to get a feel for group interaction, style of dress, general level of experience/skills, etc.

• Even if you have no desire to socialize outside of the world of mental health, develop conversational topics beyond it. And practice listening. Dale Carnegie, in *How to Win Friends and Influence People*, tells a story in which he sat next to someone at a dinner party who talked non-stop about botany the entire evening. Carnegie knew little about the subject and said almost nothing, which perhaps is why his dinner neighbor later told the host how stimulating and interesting Carnegie was. Carnegie says, "And so I had him thinking of me as a good conversationalist when, in reality, I had been merely a good listener and had encouraged him to talk."

Starting a Procovery Support Group

Reminding one another of the dream that each of us aspires to may be enough for us to set each other free.
—Antoine De Saint-Exupéry

Procovering individuals may find it useful to start a support group to offer procovery-focused support and fellowship, and to share strategies, successes, and stories.

The following approaches may be helpful as a starting point:

Group mission: For example, to share ideas, inspiration, emotional support and fellowship for procovering individuals.

Meeting structure: For example, organize discussions around the strategies (chapters) for procovery in this book or any other book you might choose to use, with the objective of brainstorming ideas, experiences, and possibilities.

Starting: You might find a couple of other people who are interested in starting a group along with you and hold an organizational meeting to decide:

- a common preference for meeting time;

- frequency for meetings;

- whether the group should be mixed
  (e.g., sex, age, diagnosis);

- open meetings or members only;

- what happens with no-shows (Is it a casual drop-in group, or is there a commitment where persons need to call a contact if they are not going to show, so that no one person attends alone?);

- any costs associated with the group and how they will be funded (through a church or community or consumer group, member contributions, other sources of funding);

- if you decide to follow the chapters of this or any other book, what period of time to spend on each chapter—e.g., one chapter a week, a month, etc.—or stay with a single chapter so long as the majority find meetings are lively or fulfilling or productive; and

- whether to have refreshments (some find this disruptive, others find refreshments lighten the atmosphere).

Name for the group: Consider joining your location with the word "procovery," e.g., "Madison Procovery."

Meeting place: Consider asking libraries, medical centers, places of worship, schools, clubhouses, and community centers that might provide not only a meeting room, but printing, publicity, etc.

A little publicity: If you're looking to expand the group, radio stations and newspapers will generally make free public service announcements, or you can make a flyer announcing the group and including a meeting place, meeting time, and contact number for more information.

A few additional suggestions:

- Use co-facilitators to run the meetings, perhaps rotating month to month (which reduces the pressure on an individual facilitator in any number of ways, including the need to be there every meeting).

- Have someone act as organizer (also perhaps on a rotating basis) to make sure of things such as the availability of the meeting room, that people know when and where meetings are to be held, the topic of the meeting, and perhaps any refreshment arrangements.

- Set the topic for each meeting ahead of time, to allow individuals to think through the subject to be discussed.

- Allow a little catch-up time at the beginning or end of each meeting, perhaps with an egg timer that gets passed around the room so everyone who wants to speak has an opportunity.

- Establish that personal information is confidential to the meeting and not to be discussed outside.

- Establish a phone tree so that everyone has only one person to call when something comes up.

Seeing a Gift in the Intent
as Much as the Action

When I walk with you, I feel as if I have a flower in my buttonhole. —William Makepeace Thackeray

I would never have procovered if not for the care given me by others. They brought me tea when I was too numb to drink it. They gave me books and rented movies when my mind was too busy to follow them. They said the "wrong" things, such as, "I don't understand how, knowing you love your daughters so much, you're allowing yourself to waste away in a psychiatric ward needlessly." They visited me with ham croissant sandwiches knowing I was a vegetarian ("You need the protein, Kathleen"). They told me to "stop all this nonsense, NOW."

Others painted my toenails and gave me manicures. They brought me goodies in pink bakery boxes all tied up with string, and fashion magazines when I didn't have the energy or interest to get out of my pajamas.

And what I learned through all of this is to recognize, accept, and appreciate *any* genuine sign of caring as the generous, heaven-sent gift it is.

If I can stop one heart from breaking,
I shall not live in vain;
If I can ease one life the aching,
Or cool one pain,

Or help one fainting robin
Unto his nest again,
I shall not live in vain.
—Emily Dickinson

Procovery Notes for Consumers

❖ **Match the support you need to someone willing and able to give it.** Consider starting a list of possible supporters, people who have told you or you know would like to give you a hand—so that when something comes up you don't find yourself constantly calling the same person, the wrong person, or no person. If you can, note the kinds of support that each person is strong at.

❖ **Make a pact with supporters that they will first take care of themselves**, easing their potential guilt for saying no at times, and your potential guilt for asking. And perhaps develop a two-tiered communication system, letting supporters know whether it is a crisis or whether it is a situation in which they should feel free to be unavailable.

❖ **Particularly for individuals who have experienced trauma and/or abuse, it can be confusing at best to know how and when to grow support**, to ask and allow others to help, to know who to trust. Taking small steps can help. Share confidences slowly. Allow yourself to be more vulnerable over time.

❖ **Avoid people who, under the guise of support, try to run your life in a direction you don't care to go**—which can result in you feeling guilty for not being grateful for "support" you don't want.

❖ **Actively seeking out the right support at the particular time needed can greatly facilitate procovery.** One individual described, "My strategy now is that if I don't feel like working, I call mom or my employment specialist. My employment specialist is more lenient. She'll say something like: 'You can take a day off. That's not bad.' But my mom is very tough, so I prefer to call her. Mother will say: 'You get your buns over there . . . you gotta go.' Within a half hour, she's right. When I get there I'm fine."[1]

❖ **Support those who support you.** Sounds simple enough. But often people overlook or underappreciate the positive supporters in their lives, in lieu of chasing after people who don't offer support. It's a little bit like focusing on not being invited to a party, knowing you've had longstanding plans to go to the movies with friends that night.

❖ **A corollary to the note above: If someone has been purposefully hurtful or unhelpful in the past, don't assume that person will be different now just because you are.**

◈ **Take advantage of the power of peer support.**
Sally Zinman writes of the importance of "peer support and client-run services, a model that emerged
from activism. Though often overlooked, these are
among the most effective forms of treatment because
of their underlying philosophy: that the best helpers
are those who have experienced similar problems . . . "[2]

◈ **Consider where you might best support others.**
Support can be a two-way street. Rather than committing to something that may sound fine at the time, but
later will result in you feeling pressured, you might
offer "spontaneous" support, such as, "I'm going to the
market, are there a couple of things I can get you?" or,
"I'm doing a load of white wash, are there a few things
you'd like me to throw in?" or, "I'm making a sandwich, can I get you one too?"

◈ **Communication is about sharing—listening as
well as speaking.** Communication is also a two-way
street. Although a psychiatric diagnosis will at times
be the main focus of your life, obviously others have
their own issues to face, too.

◈ **Be clear on what you want and let others know.**

◈ **Argue an idea not a person.**

◈ **Don't discuss heated topics at heated times or at
meals or bedtimes.**

◈ **Some people seem to be always looking for an argument**. And some, no matter how much information is offered to them, continue to make stigmatizing remarks. Refuse to be baited.

Never argue with an idiot. They drag you down to their level and beat you with experience.
—Anonymous

◈ **Keep in mind that you don't always have to respond immediately to a question**. For many questions, such as "Would you like to get together this weekend?" and, "Can you work Saturday?" rather than giving an answer you might regret, you can buy yourself a little time by responding, "Can I get back to you tomorrow?" or, "I'll need a little time to consider, how about if I call you Thursday?"

◈ **Look to surround yourself with others who are where you want to be**—it can rub off.

◈ **Treating family like company and company like family can make everyone feel welcome and at ease.**

◈ **When looking to start a conversation, if you feel you have little in common with someone**, remember that by virtue of being human what we have in common vastly exceeds our differences.

◈ **Look for movies, books, and people to laugh with.**

Laughter is the shortest distance between two people.
—Victor Borge

◈ **Consider starting a "positive club,"** where members regularly share positive stories, books, jokes, skits—anything that is positive. The group and focus don't need to pertain or be limited to mental health. You could take outings, or do almost anything, but people agree to leave any negatives at home for the meeting period.

◈ **There are some hobbies that are enjoyable but costly and/or done primarily alone.** Before exploring a new hobby, you might take your budget and social objectives into consideration.

◈ **Don't confuse independence with living alone.** For some, living alone is the optimum situation, but for others, living alone is simply lonely, and a group situation may allow for both independence and a sense of connectedness.

◈ **Sometimes, when single and at a low point, individuals feel lonely, vulnerable, and miserable and feel the solution is to be part of a couple.** Then when the resulting relationship founders, it is blamed on the impossibility of Mr. or Ms. Right, the impossibility of romantic love. In fact, as Nathaniel

Branden writes in *The Psychology of Romantic Love,* "[S]urely the error lies not in the *ideal* of romantic love, but in the irrational and impossible demands made of it." Initiating a romantic relationship at a particularly vulnerable time can play havoc with your heart. Consider waiting, on the theory that relationships are stronger when both people are independent and together interdependent. Then, when you run into difficulty, it is easier to understand that difficulty as the process of building love rather than as evidence of the impossibility of finding love.

◈ **Dating rejection**. Sometimes the things you regret in life are the things you didn't do rather than things you did. Even if you have felt unsuccessful at dating in the past, keep on trying; *increase the odds*. Reggie Jackson, one of baseball's all-time career home-run kings was also baseball's all-time career strikeout leader. Try doing new things with new people. Your past does not have to equal your future.

◈ **Don't fall into thinking that you cannot date without money**. Be creative. Can't afford to eat out? Two peanut butter sandwiches spread on a blanket at a local park can be more memorable than a five-star restaurant.

◈ **When looking to start a conversation, ask openended questions (cannot be answered with a yes**

or no). For instance, rather than, "Do you play raquetball?" try, "What do you like to do for fun?"

◈ **Life—be in it!** Get out there, find things you like to do and you'll also find people you like to be with.

Procovery Notes for Family Members

◈ **When possible, try to move forward despite differences**, rather than getting backlogged in old baggage —focusing on what to do about it now, today, rather than on the history of the problem. If the issue is someone forgetting to take their medication, and it happens again and again and leads to a crisis, it may be more productive to focus on the latest situation alone, its impact, and what might be helpful for the next time (e.g., would you like me to help you establish a reminder routine?).

◈ **One person might find it endearing that someone wants him or her to "check in" frequently, but another might find it suffocating.** What one person views as possessive, or needy, or a sign of distrust, another finds to be a sign of support and caring. There is no wrong or right; these are personal preferences that should be discussed and where necessary compromised.

◈ **Separate the person from the disorder.** Love the person, even if you hate the disorder.[3]

◈ **Take a class together** in assertiveness training or anger or communications, or perhaps an art class.

◈ **Offer to locate, test-run, or sometimes provide transportation for social activities.**

◈ **Avoid discussing heated issues at heated times, as well as at meal times and bedtimes.**

◈ **Consider holding regularly scheduled family meetings.** Setting aside a specific time for communication among family members can make the rest of the week run smoother. Rather than frequent, perhaps nit-picking or negative confrontations, issues can be addressed at an agreed-upon time. At these meetings, it can help to do the following:

• Agree on a length of time for meetings, and stick to it;

• Have each person arrive having thought through his or her priorities and problems, and *possible solutions or compromises;*

• Agree on a specific amount of time for each family member to discuss his or her priorities;

• Attend meetings with an open mind and be willing to compromise; and

• Plan ahead for unwinding time, so that meetings don't end abruptly and perhaps adversarially—

maybe with a nice dessert, a rented movie, or a walk.

◈ **Spread support around, so that no one person wears too thin**. Many times, it doesn't occur to people to offer support, but they would be pleased to respond to a specific request.

◈ **Similarly, when you offer support, it can help to be specific**. You might ask, "Is there anything I can do for you?" and receive the response, "Hey if I knew what I needed right now, I'd do it myself!" Examples of specific offers are: "Can I get you a sandwich?" or, "Would you like to take a walk together?" or, "Would you like a foot massage?" or, "Want to go get some coffee together?" or, "Would you like me to attend your doctor appointment with you today?"

◈ **When I was in the hospital, many people carried on small talk that made me feel worse**, such as, "Did you hear Beth got married?" or, "Henry started first grade," or, "John died." This made me feel more alone, more isolated. It drove the feeling home, that others' lives were moving on and mine was not. On the other hand, my mother never discussed time-line issues, but made me comfortable that life was waiting for me. She'd say things like, "I found the best new coffee, you've got to try it," or, "A new little café opened up, I can't wait to take you there," and she'd describe the café, or she would tell me funny things customers at her job had said that day.

Often communication can be facilitated by allowing for indirect eye contact and time to think and respond. Jigsaw puzzles, beeswax or modeling clay, making a collage, making sub sandwiches or pizza, and other simple activities can be conversation starters and maintainers.

Family members often feel helpless, due both to the diagnosis itself and to their lack of control in dealing with treatment in a way that they feel would be most effective. It is important not to confuse being able to cure someone with being able to help someone's healing process.

What did you like to do together before illness came into the picture? What new things might you now explore? Don't let mental illness be your sole focus. Be sure to do some enjoyable things together, such as collage, photo albums, woodworking, website building, watercolor, auto maintenance, knitting, cooking, or chess.

Procovery Notes for Staff

This chapter largely focuses on support and communications outside the treatment arena. See the chapter on partnering for communications and support tips from a treatment perspective.

Staff members often seek tangible signs they are helping. (Who wouldn't?) Recognize that many times the seeds planted don't sprout for weeks or months or years, and as noted earlier, that faith in the possibility of procovery can be self-fulfilling.

Staff must gather support, too. Brainstorm with others about what works, what doesn't work; what instills hope, what doesn't; how to feel fulfilled on unfulfilling days; and to remind each other of the long view.

"Therapists working in [abuse] situations hear story after story of human suffering. At first the stories inspire sympathy, generosity, and a passionate commitment to reducing human violence and destructiveness. But if they witness too much pain for too long, therapists who work with people who've been abused can themselves become hopeless and despairing . . . Yet . . . (w)hen practitioners meet regularly to sigh together, complain together, even shed a few tears together, and also to share their successes, they usually feel stronger." —Paul Rogat Loeb, *Soul of a Citizen*

Not all treatment discussions should center on the diagnosis. Just as some small talk takes place when you visit your doctor for a sore throat, some non-mental health topic should be brought up.

Let consumers and family members know what is available within the community, both in and out of the area of mental health.

Be supportive of clear and direct communication.
For example, "I really appreciate your clear descriptions of what helps and what doesn't," or, "It is extremely helpful that you arrive here so prepared and organized about your symptoms and priorities."

The power of "we" is huge if it really means "we."
"We need to take our meds," when only one person has to take them, is condescending and separating. On the other side, "Let's see what we can do," or, "We need to call the hospital tomorrow to get this corrected," communicates that a staffer is in it *with* the consumer. This can make an enormous difference in the often shattering loneliness of the treatment experience.

1. Alverson, M., Becker, D., and Drake, R. (1995). "An ethnographic study of coping strategies used by people with severe mental illness participating in supported employment," *Psychosocial Rehabilitation Journal*, 18(4):115-128.

2. Zinman, Sally (1999). "Treatment by Force is an Attack on Rights," *San Jose Mercury News,* June 20, 1999, Section C.

3. Sibling, Rex. *60 tips on coping with mental illness in the family*, NAMI Sibling and Adult Children Network.

Sticking With Procovery When the Going Gets Rough

We do not remember days, we remember moments.
—Cesare Pavese

Crises and relapse provide key trigger moments both in treatment and in life. To paraphrase Jerome Frank, M.D., a crisis can inspire a consumer to rise to a new solution. Or it can cause him to get worse or flee.[1]

Using crises to move toward procovery requires a reorientation in thinking, to see crisis not as an evidence of failure but as *a painful but expected part of the path to procovery, when procovery efforts can have the greatest impact.*

With this reorientation in thinking, there is a tremendous opportunity to "just start anywhere" and take procovery-oriented steps before, during, and after crises. These steps can make the difference whether a particular relapse is a detour on the way to procovery, a turning point toward procovery, or a loss of will in getting there at all.

Crises and Relapse Are Part of the Path to Procovery

My life is full of mistakes. They're like pebbles that make a good road. —Beatrice Wood

Stories abound that when consumers backslide and/or are in crisis, they are punished by the system or made to feel worse. This tendency to view all crises and relapse as an indication of failure is a serious mistake.

First, as noted elsewhere in this book, procovery, like most of life, can be two steps forward and one back, or sometimes one step forward and two back. We don't expect someone to learn to drive a car or ski on the expert slope on their first, second, or third effort; it would be equally ridiculous to expect an individual to procover from serious mental illness without setbacks or relapses. Backsliding is to be expected in any really difficult matter; it can be an indication of the difficulty of the task.

Second, often what might appear to be backsliding or "failure" is instead an integral part of the procovery process. Suppose someone has been resigned to a life of surviving at best, convinced that there is very little in life worth acting on, but then begins the process of procovery. Trying new things. Going new places. Moving. Getting a job. Like the gymnast reaching for a new skill who falls in the process, a consumer may find himself falling from time to time, perhaps needing to access crisis care three or four times in short succession. To some with a short-term focus, this might appear clinically negative; but in fact this may well be a clinically positive step toward healing.

If you haven't been working out for 15 years and start doing so at a local gym, you will initially be sore. You might pull a muscle or injure your back. You might need to access more medical care at first than you have altogether in the past 15 years. And yet ultimately you are becoming stronger and healthier, moving toward needing *less* care.

It is easy, when dealing with the pain and urgency of relapse, to forget crises are not necessarily a sign of impending doom, but at times the essential darkness before dawn.

With this orientation that crises are often not failure points but progress points, and *always* a point where procovery can begin or be fostered, consumers, family members, and treating professionals can make major changes in their approach to accept and prepare for crises, and respect what can be accomplished during them.

Crises Can Be Times of Maximum Motivation

Where there is ruin, there is hope for a treasure. —Rumi

Crisis is a time of enormous pain and urgency, and can be a time of heightened focus and potential. Much of what is often done in psychiatric crises (e.g., involuntary commitment, forced medication, seclusion, and restraints) causes long-term repercussions in the name of short-term stabilization.

Like the stories of travelers trapped in avalanches who harness never-before-found strength and courage, the enormity of the moment and the intense response to fear and pain can be a point of incredible motivation. Ironically, many say that individuals in crisis are not motivated to procover, not "procovery ready." The truth is that many individuals in psychiatric crises are highly motivated, desperate for anything that will ease their overwhelming fear and pain.

Yet often lost in the preoccupation with emergency stabilization is any effort to tap this motivation by communicating that a crisis is temporary, that things are going to get better, or by introducing procovery-oriented steps that can be continued or built upon post-crisis.

In an acute-care situation, crisis treatment may appropriately have stabilization as its dominant goal. But for individuals with chronic illness, crisis treatment is an occasional way station during a long-term treatment ride—and a primary goal must be to treat in such a way as to enhance the long-term treatment process. Failure to focus on the steps necessary for this goal not only misses a huge opportunity to bring about healing but can cause long-term damage to treatment.

Although procovery can be hugely detoured during crises, procovery seeds can be planted there as well. Procovery-oriented actions can turn this time of maximum risk into critical turning points toward healing.

Preventing and Planning for Crises

I'm no longer afraid of storms, for I am learning how to sail my own ship. —Louisa May Alcott

Obviously, preventing a fire is best; putting it out early is second best. Similarly, preventing or minimizing a crisis is hugely beneficial. And yet, when numbing feelings of depression or any other warning signs surface, the emotions themselves may make it difficult to take the necessary steps. The reverse is also true; when someone is feeling on top of the world, he or she may give little thought to preventing illness.

To manage crises *before* they occur:

Develop a relapse prevention plan. The objective is to identify a toolbox of steps, when warning signs surface, that you might try or have previously identified as helpful. It is likely best done in writing, shared with your supporters. Such a plan will get better with experience, as an individual learns what works best over time. It might be calling a support person and letting him or her know what is happening (beginning to feel manic or depressed, hearing voices, etc.); calling a crisis line; pulling out a hope or procovery journal; increasing your lighting whether by indoor halogen light or going out for a walk; deep breathing or relaxation techniques; or taking additional medication prescribed specifically for times of crisis.

Develop a crisis management plan. Identify in advance symptoms that are likely indicators you are in crisis; people who you want to make decisions and advocate on your behalf; medications that have proved to be successful in the past and those that have an allergic or other negative impact; physical issues such as chronic pain, low blood sugar, high blood pressure, headaches, back pain; facilities where you would wish to receive treatment and where you wouldn't; treating professionals you have had success in working with and any you have not.

Acting Rather Than Reacting During a Crisis

Kind words can be short and easy to speak, but their echoes are truly endless. —Mother Teresa

Many think that a procovery approach has no place during times of crisis. And yet, crisis isn't some whole other separate location off the healing path; instead it can be an intimate and integral part of what is often a winding path to procovery. Clearly, in view of limited resources, timing matters. For example, a supportive employment program will likely be significantly more effective *after* a crisis has passed. But procovery can and should be fueled at all times, particularly in times of crisis.

Although there are many places for a consumer to be proactive in preventing and managing crises, once a crisis becomes full-blown, oftentimes fuel for procovery needs to come more from the outside—that is, staff and loved ones—than from the individual in crisis.

What can staff and loved ones do? As with much of procovery, the first step is a reorientation of focus. In addition to asking the basic question, "How can this person be most effectively stabilized?" loved ones and treating professionals need to ask two more questions:

What can I do to avoid unnecessarily escalating the crisis? If someone is having a heart palpitation and you respond, "Oh my God, he's having a heart attack," that is unlikely to help. Anger, panic, and other responses to the frightening aspects of psychiatric crises can cause even greater fear and paralysis for an individual in crisis, and lead to a worsening spiral. Learn over time what responses reduce or escalate crises for a specific individual.

Are there procovery seeds that I can plant, knowing I might never see them grow? Procovery seeds planted during times of crisis often take deepest root. Times of crisis can be key leverage points to communicate essential principles of procovery—that procovery is possible, that individuals can heal despite lack of a cure, and that it can help to focus on what we can do, with what we have now.

Here are nine strategies staff and loved ones can use (just starting anywhere!) to move an individual in crisis toward procovery:

Offer choice to the extent possible. Even in the most extreme circumstances there are often choices.

Be creative. Is there a possible choice for a medication to be delivered orally or by injection? Could it be given now or in two minutes? The value of offering choice in procovery is immeasurable. Even if an individual doesn't respond, it often registers that he or she is with someone he or she can trust on some level, is being treated respectfully, and is a welcome part of his or her own healing process. Simple examples: "Is there someone you'd like us to call?" or, "What do you feel you need to feel better?" or, "We're focusing on getting you stabilized and then we'd like to talk about your various treatment choices."

Communicate. At the very least, staff should tell consumers what they are doing and why. And consumers should if possible let people know if there is someone they want to be called, if they have an advance directive, and if there is anything in particular that helps or doesn't.

Consider physical as well as mental health issues. It is critical to recognize and treat the interactions between physical and mental health issues, whether those interactions are due to the nature of the illness (such as chronic pain and depression) or the nature of the treatment (such as side effects to medications). In this vein, communication with other treating staff, such as primary care and general practitioners, is important.

Remember the importance of the ordinary.
Because of the natural tendency to assume that big
problems require big solutions, everyday human needs
can easily be minimized. The irony is that particularly
in times of crisis, small acts of compassion loom larger
than ever, whether it is a squeeze of the hand, using
the person's first name, adjusting clothing that may be
caught up, or offering a drink of water.

Don't punish for being in crisis. Individuals sometimes receive punishment or reduced care because
they are in crisis; in fact they need more care, not less.
For example, seclusion and restraints, controversial
control techniques, have been used as a punishment.
Betty Blaska, M.A., wrote, "We ask you to see us in
seclusion and restraint as you would see a non-mental
health consumer in an ICU (intensive care unit). We
are in pain, having acute crisis, very much injured
and hurt; we are *injured*, not *bad*; we need *more* not
less attention in S & R."[2]

Employ the power of we. Crises can be devastating
in part because of the overwhelming loneliness experienced. Never underestimate the "power of we" to
impact this loneliness. For example, "Together we'll
get you through this," or, "Let's see what we can do to
get you feeling better," or, "Together we'll give it a
shot."

Exercise rational instead of irrational authority.
As noted in the chapter of this book on medication

management, Erich Fromm distinguishes "irrational authority," which is based on power and creates further dependence, from "rational authority," which is based on competence and helps the person who leans on it to grow (and tends to dissolve itself as it achieves its goal). In crisis, staff have maximum power and authority; it is therefore the most critical time for staff to consider, when doing something invasive or unwanted, "Is what I am doing absolutely necessary?" and "Is there any way I can do something *with* this person rather than *to* this person?"

Avoid re-traumatizing. Many individuals served by mental health systems have experienced trauma and/or abuse, including domestic abuse, sexual abuse, sexual assault, war, or other types of extreme violence on the body or soul, including trauma caused by past mental health treatment. Recognize that crisis can be a result of, and/or trigger for, overwhelming memories and feelings of past trauma. A major risk in crisis treatment for these persons is re-traumatization.

Think of a woman who has been sexually abused, who finds herself in crisis, in a psychiatric hospital. Common actions taken by staff in efforts to stabilize the individual can be similar to those taken by a past abuser, and as a result will likely not stabilize but rather escalate the crisis. Being taken down, stripped with legs spread in restraints by male attendants— these and other actions can serve as vicious reminders of past violations and significantly intensify the crisis.[3]

Build hope and a vision of procovery. Consumers tell stories of small acts of compassion and belief that the future will be better that, unknown to the person building the hope, months or years later were recognized as having been critical turning points in procovery.

Suicide

Suicide is a particularly awful way to die: the mental suffering leading up to it is usually prolonged, intense, and unpalliated. —Kay Redfield Jamison

Suicide is less an act than a tale of the soul.
—M. Jouhandeau

Suicide is an often-misunderstood risk, hopelessly entangled in illness, in faith, in guilt, in myth. It is essential to dispel certain myths, in order to get past these entanglements to the real object, stopping preventable suicide.

Myth: Suicide is the easy way out, done in a rash moment.

Many view suicide as the easy way out. Although it is true that suicide places the pain of an individual on the shoulder of loved ones, suicide is never easy. And generally, in the case of an individual diagnosed with mental illness, it's been a long time in coming.

There is a story that Picasso, out to dinner, was interrupted by a fellow diner who asked that he "doodle" for her on a napkin, and that she would pay what Picasso felt fair.

And he did. She then asked how much she should pay, and he said $15,000. "Fifteen thousand dollars!" she shrieked. "For three minutes of work?" "Ah madam," he said, "three minutes and 20 years."

Suicide committed by individuals with chronic mental illness is less likely the rash act of three minutes than a tragic consequence of chronic mental illness. Suicide isn't easy, ever, not for the one who acts or the ones who are left.

Myth: Suicide is a selfish act.

Often individuals who commit suicide think they are offering the finest and only gift they have. That without them in the way, their families can move on, regroup, and have a non-hellish life. It can weigh heavily to know the pain your illness is causing your loved ones. Guilt is often a part of the reason for suicide. It feels awful to see oneself as a forever burden to others. Suicide for these individuals is a result of a hellish illness, not selfishness.

Myth: Those who talk about suicide aren't at risk of doing it.

Many believe that those who talk about suicide are just talking, that they won't really act on it. Unfortunately, many individuals, after weeks (or months or years) of talking about suicide, take their own life. Suicide talk should always be taken seriously.

Myth: Individuals only commit suicide when things are at their worst.

Sometimes, when things appear to be going best, individuals become suicidal, and others are dumbfounded, remarking that "things are going so well, why now?" The fact is that sometimes when things are said to be "at their best," it can be a time when an individual may decide, "If this is as good as it gets, it isn't good enough. If it's the best I can hope for, why go on?"

To the outsider, an individual who spends years to finally stabilize on a med and a job may have reached success. But this is likely a critical time to help the individual understand that those successes are not "as good as it gets," but are an indication of the continued possibilities on the path to procovery.

Diseases can be our spiritual flat tires—disruptions in our lives that seem to be disasters at the time but end by redirecting our lives in a meaningful way.
—Bernie Siegel, M.D.

Procovery Notes for Consumers

❖ **Together with treating professionals, create a pre-crisis plan**. When warning signs surface, there may be steps that you have previously identified that help. Keep a reminder of these steps anywhere easy to access (perhaps on the refrigerator), that can identify what to do when things start to get out of hand. For example, if you are becoming depressed, your reminder might say, "If you are depressed and can leave the house, go for a walk. If you can't get out of the house, play Pachelbel's Canon and turn on ALL the lights. Do NOT call so and so, or have a drink . . . " You are the expert on what works for you; in the area of prevention this is a critical advantage.

A wise man lowers a ladder before he goes into a pit.
—Folk saying

❖ **Know what to do in a crisis**. Crises are key trigger points both in treatment and in life. The delicate balance in which we live can be destroyed by not knowing what to do.

Spend a few minutes with your psychiatrist developing a crisis plan—whom you would call, during and outside of office hours, in what order, and what facility to go to.

Consider also agreeing on specific words to use. Crisis is a challenging time for anyone to communicate—for some it is impossible. Emergency personnel can have a difficult time determining how best to help when consumers are unable to express important information about their history or symptoms. Having these words available, in writing if necessary, can make a critical difference in the quality of intervention.

Write this plan down and put it somewhere easily accessible to you and anyone advocating on your behalf, including perhaps your doctor.

◈ **Consider the use of an advance directive** to manage your crisis care. Include information as to past trauma, medications and other treatments that help and hurt, and individuals who you want to advocate for you when you are unable to do so for yourself. (See the Procovery Note for Consumers, "Complete an advance directive," in the partnering chapter.)

◈ **Your best advocate is not necessarily the person who loves you the most.** The best advocate is someone who knows how to advocate for you the best! Select someone who is assertive, communicates well, and works toward getting you where *you* want to go.

◈ **Find at least one 24-hour crisis line.** As one individual states, "I was locked up against my will twice last year. Both times I just needed someone to talk to. But now another consumer told me about a crisis hotline . . . "[4]

◈ **Don't put the brakes on when you're at a dip in the roller coaster ride.** People in crisis tend to think what's happening right now is the way things will stay. Try to remind yourself that life is long and a crisis temporary.

◈ **Possible calming techniques**: Music, aromatherapy, bubble baths, breathing exercises, relaxation and meditation techniques, stress balls. Consider whether a change in lighting is helpful to you during crises. Some feel safest and least likely to harm themselves in their bed in a darkened room; for others, this is the worst thing they could do, as they would likely have an increase in hearing voices, disorganized thinking, fear, etc.

◈ **Talk to your doctor as to whether a small increase in medication might be prescribed in advance**, by a separate prescription, for your use during times of crisis.

◈ **It is almost impossible when in crisis to tell yourself not to think thoughts that escalate the crisis, but you often can refocus** on something else and achieve the same result. For example, rather than thinking and rethinking about the possibility of hospitilization that terrifies you, refocus your thinking on your hope journal, or how a support person is on his way over, or how your medication should soon take effect.

◈ **Try not to let a crisis escalate; take the early steps you know will help**. Just like momentum builds on itself, crisis can build upon itself and become paralyzing. There is often a window of time, before a crisis escalates to a catastrophic level, when you know through experience what you should do. For example, a person may feel a manic phase coming on and know he or she should seek emergency care. Part of your procovery process may involve having the discipline not to opt for the future catastrophe over the action you would have to take now.

Procovery Notes for Family Members

❖ **It can be infuriating to have little control over a treatment plan and yet feel responsibility over a crisis**. This is an area where there is generally no perfect solution. It can be useful to share this concern with your loved one, but not during a time of crisis, as the discussion will not be productive at such a time. Having a treatment-planning meeting for all concerned during a relatively stable time to agree on crisis planning may help.

❖ **Do not downplay crises, but gently assure that, as overwhelming as things are, the crisis or relapse is temporary.** "I know this is a really hard time," or "I will help you get through this," (or some other pre-determined calming phrase) can help remind your loved one that a crisis is temporary, and that he or she will get through the crisis.

❖ **Never underestimate the power of we**. Crises are devastatingly lonely, terrifying times. Reminding someone that you (and other trusted support persons and professionals) are there for him or her can make all the difference. This is the power of "we." Perhaps, "Together we will make it through this crisis."

◈ **Ask your loved one what he or she feels is needed to feel better**. And honor the request if possible, whether you think it will be a benefit or not, as long as it won't harm the person. Often the request will be something simple and yet have a powerful impact.

◈ **Although privacy is essential to mental health, during times of catastrophic crisis don't leave your loved one alone**. This can be exhausting; enlist the help of others. But it is important to do this in as respectful and non-intrusive a manner as possible.

◈ **Take seriously suicidal talk and other possible warning signs**, including—making a will; getting rid of personal belongings; destroying journals; increasing use of drugs and alcohol; and uncustomary withdrawing from family, friends, and activities.

◈ **Don't argue about suicide; listen**. Allow your loved one to talk about it, providing a perhaps life-saving outlet.

◈ **For some individuals experiencing suicidal thoughts, suggesting that suicide is a sin, or selfish or immoral may increase the pressure and have just the opposite effect you intend**.

Remember that for individuals with chronic mental illness, suicide is the result of an illness and not a choice.

❖ **For some people in crisis, telling them, "It's O.K., calm down," can have a soothing effect. For others it may have just the opposite effect,** and it can be more helpful to ask them if they would like to tell you why they are in crisis. Ask your loved one, preferably during a stable time, what works best for them.

Procovery Notes for Staff

❖ **Together with a consumer, create a crisis prevention plan** (preventing a fire). See the first Procovery Note for consumers, above.

❖ **Together with a consumer, create an in-crisis plan** (extinguishing the fire early). See the second procovery note for consumers, above.

❖ **Refocusing thinking can be hugely beneficial.** Sometimes rather than asking, "Why do you want to die?" ask, "What do you have to live for?" and build on that.

Betty Blaska, M.A., described to me the time she went to a hospital emergency room in crisis, suicidal. She'd been to dozens of emergency rooms over the years, and was used to being asked why she was in crisis, why she wanted to die. But she'd never been asked and wasn't prepared for the question this emergency room doc asked her. He asked her what she had to live for. Betty was completely taken aback, and her reasons slowly came to mind—her cat, and the children she instructed in religion, her mental health advocacy work, and the people she loved—she found her focus had shifted from one of desperately wanting to die to one of thinking about life.

◈ **Ask consumers what they believe they need to feel better**. See the Family Procovery Note, above.

◈ **Be clear what to do in a crisis and whom to call, during and after office hours**. Consumers note, "Secretaries act as gatekeepers and try to protect the doctor—why not have an intermediary who can deal with us in a crisis?" "Would you please answer phone calls . . . we wait and wait and never know if you got the call. A lot of crises could be prevented."[5]

◈ **Times of crisis can conjure memories of prior crises**. Sometimes you can ease the pressure and change the focus by reminding consumers that the past does not equal the future. One way to accomplish this is to focus on what is different today from prior crises. Possibly ask, "What is different about *the situation* this time?" and, "What is different about *you* this time?" For example, perhaps the person now has been successfully through a crisis in the past, or has built more support, or knows a medication he or she responds to, or has formed a collaborative relationship with a treating professional, or is receiving care earlier than in prior crises.

❖ **Consider whether a pre-approved increase in medication—that a consumer can take at the time of early warning signs of relapse—might prevent deterioration and rehospitalization.** Ian Chovil wrote, "My psychiatrist got tired of me phoning him every time it happened and suggested I increase my medication 5 mg. when I noticed it and take a good look at what stresses and responsibilities were demanding too much from me. After a week the emergent symptoms have always faded."[6]

❖ **To the extent possible, collect information about past traumas,** both to prevent misdiagnosis and to lessen the likelihood of escalating a crisis by treatment that re-traumatizes.

❖ **Be sensitive to escalating crises of survivors of sexual abuse**: Betty Blaska, M.A., writes, "Survivors of childhood sexual abuse—very scary to have clothes taken away; incredibly unbearable to be stripped or to have hygiene done by males (with some even by females). A cardinal rule is DON'T TOUCH UNLESS ASKED/TELL FIRST. We need low, soothing, slowly speaking voices, low stimulation. If 'rushing' is necessary, let it be done by one or two, not a whole gang of male staff members."[7]

If you suspect or become aware of sexual abuse or other trauma, consider referring to a rape crisis center or other type of organization that specializes in trauma and/or abuse.

Build hope. Procovery efforts in the midst of crisis are critical. Partner and offer choice to the extent possible. Explain what you are doing and why.

1. Frank, Jerome (1974). *Persuasion and Healing*, New York: Schocken Books, p. 286.

2. Blaska, Betty (1990). "Expanded Notes from Mendota Training Seclusion & Restraint," *Emerging Force*, July/Aug 1994.

3. Ann Jennings, Ph.D., has crafted an excellent table comparing early childhood trauma experiences with common mental health institutional practices. "On Being Invisible In the Mental Health System" in *Women's Mental Health Services: A Public Health Perspective*, Levine, Bruce L., Blanch, Andrea K., Jennings, Ann, eds. Contact: Ann Jennings, Office of Trauma Services, Department of Mental Health, Mental Retardation, and Substance Abuse Services, 40 State House Station, Augusta, ME 04333-0040; 207-287-4250; and see www.umaine.edu/sws/ots.

4. Exchange, *Health Action Letter:When Choices are Limited*, Health Action Network, San Francisco, California.

5. Exchange, *Health Action Letter:When Choices are Limited*, Health Action Network, San Francisco, California.

6. Chovil, Ian (1999). *Relapse Prevention*, www.chovil.com/prevention.html.

7. Blaska, Betty (1990). "Expanded Notes from Mendota Training Seclusion & Restraint," *Emerging Force*, July/Aug 1994.

Self-Care: Actions to Take and Choices to Make

A student asked a wise man the secret of life. The wise man answered that there are two dogs inside of each man, a good one, and a bad one, fighting. 'Which one wins?' asked the student. 'It depends,' answered the wise man, 'which one you feed the most.'

Hans Selye, M.D., defined disease as a continuing internal struggle between the forces of illness and an individual's defenses. He wrote in *The Stress of Life* that "this is an important point and one which, despite being constantly rediscovered during the intervening centuries, is not yet generally understood even today. Disease is not a mere surrender to attack but also fight for health; unless there is fight there is no disease."

In the context of procovery, overcoming chronic illness does not require vanquishing the forces of illness. Instead, the illness may remain and the fight continue, but the body and spirit are sufficiently reinforced so that the ongoing battle does not materially detract from the opportunity to live a productive and fulfilling life.

This is where self-care comes in: tools and habits that fuel the fight.

Self-care is particularly important for individuals diagnosed with psychiatric disorders, for two reasons. First,
the narrowing focus of mental health treatment and
research on pharmaceuticals increases the importance of
employing self-care strategies. Notes Jerry Dincin, Ph.D.,
"Known medications unfortunately do not work for some
people, or they work only modestly or engender an allergic
response, leaving people with too many symptoms to operate effectively. . . . Just as frustrating is the situation of
the people for whom medications work well initially but
then lose effectiveness over time."[1]

Second, the pricing and profit pressures on most health
care organizations limit treatment alternatives even further. Medications must be not only therapeutically *effective* but therapeutically *efficient*.[2] Further, many treatment services are required to focus on those that can
deliver *measurable outcomes in the short-term*, to match
the health care provider contract terms. Until these
organizations are able to extend their financial horizon
past next year's contract renewal, or the next shareholder
quarterly report, many of the longer-term needs of procovering individuals will go unaddressed within the system.

What Is Self-care?

*The spirit of self-help is the root of all genuine growth in
the individual; and, exhibited in the lives of many, it con-
stitutes the true source of national vigor and strength.
Help from without is often enfeebling in its effects, but help
from within invariably invigorates.* —Samuel Smiles (1859)

"Self-care" carries widely different meanings to different people. For this book, self-care refers to taking advantage of what is available *outside of the mental health care system*, including complementary medicine, self-help strategies, and community resources.

How To Approach Self-care

The more serious the illness, the more important it is for you to fight back, mobilizing all your resources—spiritual, emotional, intellectual, physical.
—Norman Cousins

Approaching self-care is like approaching procovery in general—a matter of setting favorable conditions and then selecting a strategy to try, recognizing that you can just start anywhere and in any increment.

What are key favorable conditions?

Give it time. For self-care to be effective, we need to give it time; the benefit generally won't occur overnight. Some research indicates an action has to be repeated for three weeks to even begin to become a habit, and as far as obvious therapeutic benefit goes, it can take longer.

Believe in it. Belief in a self-care strategy can be a major factor in its effectiveness. This is both because of the biological impact of expectations[3] and the increased likelihood of follow through.[4] For this reason, one should focus on self-care choices that specifically take into account personal considerations such as interests, beliefs, strengths, finances, and risk tolerance.

Go where the energy is. As Eric Hoffer has said, "Men weary as much of not doing the things they want to do as of doing the things they do not want to do." When looking at self-care alternatives, consider not only what might be a *beneficial* thing for you to do but also what might be an *energizing* thing for you to do. What will make you want to get out of bed in the morning? If you begin by doing something that gives you energy and hope, you will be receiving a therapeutic benefit from the start.

Just start anywhere in any amount. You don't have to reach for perfection. Some experts would have us believe that, whether it's exercise, diet, light, or vitamin supplements, if we don't get or do or take just the right amount, our efforts will be of no benefit. In reality, this is not the case. Nathaniel Hawthorne said, "We go all wrong by too strenuous a resolution to go all right." In trying to follow the perfect action plan it is easy to become frustrated and give up on any action at all.

Keep treating professionals advised of self-care approaches you are considering. Given the explosion of information on self-care alternatives, and the scarcity of funding for clinical research on those alternatives, it is possible that your treating professional will be unable to advise you on whether a particular self-care approach will help. But he may be able to advise you whether it is likely to *harm* you. For example, individuals taking lithium who exercise can get dehydrated and become toxic. For another example, the amino acid dl-phenylalanine (also called DLPA), available widely at health food stores, was remarkably effective for both my depression and chronic pain. However you should not take DLPA in a number of circumstances, including if you are pregnant, breast-feeding, have high blood pressure, are taking MAOIs (monoamine oxidase inhibitors), or have diabetes or phenylketonuria (the inability to convert phenylalanine into another amino acid, tyrosine).[5]

Putting Together a Personal Toolbox

If the only tool you have is a hammer, you're going to treat everything as if it were a nail. —Pavlov

It would be nice if there were *one* answer to feeling better. One exercise to do, or one pill to take. However, one generally reaches procovery through an accumulation of helpful things, both actions to take and choices to make.

Years ago, each new thing I tried struck me as time-consuming, tiring, and complicated. I felt angry that, even if it ultimately helped, I would have to continue any number of tiresome actions for months or years or even permanently. I felt annoyed that I had to make any effort at all. But now, years later, I have put together a collection of things that help me, a personal toolbox of self-care steps that I can choose from and rely on. And that I generally don't think twice about or even realize I am doing.

One's ability to adjust to life over time is remarkable, as the initially insurmountable becomes routine.

Actions To Take

I read and walked for miles at night along the beach, writing bad blank verse and searching endlessly for someone wonderful who would step out of the darkness and change my life. It never crossed my mind that person could be me.
—Anna Quindlen

Our mothers were right. Sleeping, eating, exercise, and other daily habits do make a difference. Although none of these may be the elusive cure, and no one solution may exist, along the way many of these seemingly small things can have a positive impact and ultimately snowball into procovery.

Listed below are major self-care areas from which to choose (see the Procovery Notes to this chapter for specific suggestions in each of the areas):

Sleeping—Sleep deprivation can be so serious that Amnesty International considers it a form of torture.[6] Simple improvements in sleeping habits can make a material difference in your body's ability to heal; taking steps to sleep restfully can be a significant contributor to procovery.

Eating—Eating habits affect mood, energy, and sleep quality, and the impact can be intensified by many medications. For example, many psychiatric medications cause individuals to crave carbohydrates, often leading to increased eating and weight gain, and decreased energy, activity, and self-esteem.

Exercise—Although experts debate the optimum time and frequency for exercise, in truth any increase can be helpful (check with your physician first). Shortly after I started an exercise program, I was complaining to my daughter Amanda that I just hated it. She exclaimed, "I know, but the thing is the more you exercise the more you want to!" Her enthusiasm sold me, and I found it was a matter of getting started and keeping with it until it became a habit. Then I found Amanda was right. Soon I really looked forward to the way exercising made me feel afterward.

Light—As with exercise, experts debate the optimum amount and type, but any increase in natural or artificial light can help. I have begun thinking of storing light in the pineal gland (a pine-cone shaped gland located in the middle of the brain that among many other things affects mood and sleeping) as like putting money in the bank!

Inactivity—This is a hugely important issue and needs to be addressed in a broad manner, as inactivity tends to build on itself and can further a destructive cycle of illness. People often don't think of inactivity as a problem in itself, rather they see it as a by-product (e.g., tired because of their meds, or because of their depression, or because they aren't getting any exercise). Any break in the cycle of activity can have a profound ripple effect, either way—which is why self-care is so important in breaking the cycle of illness.

Complementary medicine and health store products—The absence of clinical research on the vast array of non-pharmaceutical options—frequently lumped together as "complementary medicine"—makes it difficult for many doctors to recommend non-pharmaceutical approaches. Whether the lack of research is due to a lack of profit potential or a lack of therapeutic potential is a matter of controversy. Many individuals report significant therapeutic benefit from complementary medicine techniques such as acupuncture, acupressure, massage, chiropractics, and biofeedback, some of which may be available for the asking in health plans.

Health store vitamin supplements have been helpful for many individuals. For example, it has been reported that Vitamin E can be effective in reducing tardive dyskinesia (involuntary, repetitive movement induced by long-term use of anti-psychotic agents);[7] Vitamin B-3 in aiding schizophrenia;[8] Vitamin B-6 in helping to reduce dry mouth and urination problems caused by tricyclic antidepressants;[9] and St. John's Wort in treating depression (not to be taken in conjunction with certain prescribed antidepressants).[10]

Undressing stress—Identifying and having an impact on some of the stressors in daily life, and utilizing various relaxation techniques (including breathing exercises, meditation and aromatherapy) to absorb some of the stress that cannot be eliminated, can substantially aid every other aspect of healing.

Choices To Make

Self-care is living with an attitude. —Gilberto Romero

Self-care is not only available through actions but also through everyday choices in how you live, what you do, and whom you do it with. Here are some examples:

Activities you enjoy—If you have no reason to get out of bed, you're less likely to do so. The most "therapeutic" activities are often the ones we escape into, losing our sense of time, consumed by what we are doing. These activities vary greatly for individuals, whether it is finding a tiny plot of dirt to start a garden, taking a walk in a local park, feeding the ducks, volunteering at a food pantry, trying a new recipe, or attending a support group or poetry reading.

It is difficult to get the news from poems;
Yet men die miserably every day for lack
Of what is found there.
  —William Carlos Williams

Home as haven—Whether a large house, a small apartment, or a shared dorm room, the ability to make it special, inviting, and personal matters. A personal haven to escape to and rely on (and sometimes just the dream of such a haven) can pull an individual through hectic days and dark times. In *Rachel and Her Children*, Jonathan Kozol writes of a homeless woman's vision of such a haven:

> Last night I had a dream of an apartment. It was so real I keep on thinking that I went there in my sleep. My daughter had her own room, pink and white with something up over the bed. A canopy is what it's called, I think . . . The boys, they had to share a room. I painted that room blue; there was a spread over the bed that Doby slept in. It had football pictures on it. My kitchen had a phone, a stove, refrigerator, toaster, all of those nice things. My dining-room table was glass and it was simple, plain and clean. In my living room I had a pretty couch and lots of books, a big bookshelf, and there were plants beside the window, and the floor was what I call a parquet floor and it was waxed. My bedroom had a nice brass bed, a lot of books there too, and pillows covered with fresh linens, and the drapes were nice bright colors. Yellow. Like the linens. And the neighborhood was clean. The neighborhood was nice. The neighbors liked me. And the landlord liked me too. He said that we could use the backyard, so we bought a grill to barbecue outside on summer nights. Then I woke up.

This can remind all of us to dream of the haven we can create, as well as to make better use of whatever haven we might have.

Watching who you spend your time with—Some people will give you energy. Some will take it away. The former are better. Be careful of the "hope busters" and "energy vacuums" out there who will suck you dry if you let them.

Helping others—It helps us heal.

Listen to the inner voice that urges you, in the midst of suffering, to reach out to someone else who is also suffering. It is one of the great antidotes to the self-absorption that physical illness and emotional pain can bring and, I am sure, one of the powerful individual and collective healing mechanisms that NATURE has programmed into us. —James Gordon, M.D.

Procovery Notes for Consumers

❖ **Try one new self-care strategy at a time**, unless multiple strategies specifically work in conjunction with each other (such as certain vitamins that should be taken together). Trying several new self-care strategies at once can make it difficult to assess or determine which might be helpful. Start slow and build on successes.

❖ **Make your home your haven**. People are sensitive to their environment in different ways: light, airflow, noise, temperature, color, organization. Many of these sensitivities are believed to have biological impacts. For example, in *Prescription for Nutritional Healing (2d ed.)* it is noted that "[a]ccording to Dr. Alexander Schauss, director of the American Institute for Biosocial Research in Tacoma, Washington, when the energy of color enters our bodies, it stimulates the pituitary and pineal glands. This in turn affects the production of certain hormones, which in turn affect a variety of physiological processes. This explains why color has been found to have such a direct influence on our thoughts, moods, and behavior."

❖ **Break the cycle of inactivity**. To do this just start anywhere—sleeping, eating, exercise, lighting, etc. Something as simple as taking a walk can have a ripple effect—increasing the light in your pineal glands, which increases your ability to sleep better that night, which increases your energy the next day, which increases the likelihood you might exercise the next day, which increases your production of endorphins, which increases your feeling of hope, and so on.

❖ **Exercise**. Dr. Andrew Weil states, "Aerobic exercise is actually the best antidepressant I know, provided it is done vigorously enough and often enough. In addition to its many well-known effects on the body, it increases production of endorphins, the brain's own opiate-like molecules that are associated with some of our best natural highs."[11]

◈ **Eating**. It can be helpful to reduce any chronic habits of caffeine, alcohol, smoking, or sweets. But overall, you might focus less on the bad food you eat than the good food. Are you eating more sweets than you think you should? Increase your fruits, vegetables, and grains, for the double benefit of increased nutritional value and a likely decrease in your appetite for sweets.

◈ **Light**. Natural outdoor sunlight is best and full spectrum artificial lighting can be a close second, but in truth any increase can be a factor in improving sleep, energy, and moods. Halogen lighting, which is a clean white light, can work exceptionally well.

◈ **Sleep**. Find and focus on getting your right level of sleep. In addition, Michael Norton, M.D., has excellent recommendations for "sleep hygiene"[12] including:

• Use the bedroom only for sleeping and sex;

• Set a time for going to bed and a time for rising that stays the same weekdays and weekends;

• Develop a relaxing bedtime routine;

• Exercise regularly, preferably in the late afternoon;

• Avoid substances that alter physical or mental states—caffeine and even cigarettes—near bedtime (among the worst is alcohol, which can disrupt sleep all night);

• Make your bedroom "sleep central," quiet and dark.

Pay attention to your bedtime reading. Read things that experience tells you will make you sleep better rather than worse.

Also, how you wake up matters. There's a reason they call it an "alarm" clock; consider whether yours is right for you. Some people need to be immediately jolted out of bed, others like to be soothed out of bed, maybe with 30 minutes of gentle snooze alarm reminders.

Remember that the shortest distance between despair and hope is often a good night's sleep.
—Hope Heart Institute

❖ **Supplements**. Consult with treating professionals before taking supplements. But keep in mind that they may not have enough information (or there simply might not be enough research) to comfortably recommend a specific supplement. Or they may have a very different slant than you on alternative treatments. Nonetheless, it is important to determine whether a specific supplement may be harmful (because of your specific symptoms, interactions with a med you are taking, etc.). So if you are eager to try something but anticipate reluctance or negativity from your treating professional, rather than asking, "Is this likely to help me?" you might ask, "Is this likely to harm me?"

◈ **Substance abuse.** As Gilberto Romero has said, "Substance abuse makes any situation worse." There are an enormous number of self-care possibilities, including:

• Seek out information and support from local 12-step support groups such as Alcoholics Anonymous (AA) and Narcotics Anonymous (NA).

• Some find *When AA Doesn't Work for You: Rational Steps to Quitting Alcohol* by Albert Ellis, Ph.D. and Emmett Velten, Ph.D., and *How Alcoholics Anonymous Failed Me: My Personal Journey to Sobriety through Self-Empowerment*, by Marianne Gillian, to be additional or alternative resources.

• Avoid known triggers. One thing often leads to another. Whether it's a cigarette leading to a drink, or a party where drugs are present leading to drug use, avoid your known triggers.

• Eliminating sugar from your diet may reduce a craving for alcohol and or drugs.[13]

• James and Phyllis Balch report that the supplement glutathione may aid in reducing the desire for drugs or alcohol. They recommend taking it with L-methionine, and specifically *not* to substitute glutamic acid for glutathione. See their book, *Prescription for Nutritional Healing* (p. 106 and 241 in the 1997 edition) for recommendations and contraindications.

- Find people who support abstaining. And by all means avoid those who don't.

❖ **Consider self-care strategies for medication side effects**. For example, for constipation:

- Dr. Andrew Weil suggests drinking more water, exercising more, drinking less caffeine, and increasing fiber;[14]

- Dr. Earl Mindell recommends water, acidophilus liquid and bran;[15] and

- James and Phyllis Balch recommend aloe vera juice, garlic, and vitamin C.[16]

As another example, for dry mouth, Dr. Weil recommends as follows:[17]

- Sip water frequently during the day, and keep a glass of water at your bedside at night.

- A little lemon juice added to your drinking water should stimulate saliva flow.

- Avoid both salty and sugary foods.

- Chew sugarless gum.

- Avoid alcohol (and mouthwashes that contain alcohol), caffeinated beverages, and tobacco.

- Use a humidifier at home.

- Try commercial saliva substitutes—available at drugstores—to help keep your mouth moist.

- Until you find a solution, make an extra effort to keep your teeth and gums in good shape. Use fluoride toothpaste and alcohol-free mouthwash to prevent plaque accumulation.

❖ **Undressing stress.** More and more we seem to save time to kill it. And to wonder what we're doing wrong when life is hard. But to a certain extent, life is . . . hard. Enjoying it despite the hardship is the secret.

- Focus more on what really matters and less on what's urgent. Don't get hung up on your telephone. Why should you jump whenever it rings? What are you, Pavlov's dog?[18]

- Respect your rhythms. Things tend to be more upsetting when you are overtired or hungry.

- Have backups. An extra key given to a trusted neighbor, extra meds kept somewhere you spend a lot of time, a tucked away $5 bill (just for emergencies!) in your wallet.

- Limit multi-tasking. That's computer talk for doing several things at once.[19]

- Allow for transition, not just for major changes, but in everyday life, such as getting up, going to bed, or coming home. It may be just a few minutes for a cup of tea, playing a musical instrument, leafing through a magazine, or doing a crossword puzzle, but the importance of transition time in reducing stress is often overlooked.

- Do something enjoyable every day with no set purpose in mind. Take a walk, watch the clouds, paint someone's toenails.

❖ **Laugh**. Build something into your day, every day, that makes you laugh. Dr. Bernie Siegel notes in *Love, Medicine and Miracles*, "There are sound, scientific reasons why we call robust, unrestrained laughter 'hearty.' It produces complete, relaxed action of the diaphragm, exercising the lungs, increasing the blood's oxygen level, and gently toning the entire cardiovascular system. Norman Cousins termed it 'internal jogging,' and others have likened it to a deep massage."

❖ **Relaxation techniques**. James and Phyllis Balch note, "A technique called progressive relaxation can be helpful. This involves tightening and relaxing the major muscle groups one at a time, being aware of each sensation. Start at your feet and work up to your head. Tense the muscles for a count of ten, concentrating on the tension, then let the muscles go lax and breathe, deeply, enjoying the sensation of release."[20]

❖ **Meditation**. There are a variety of ways to meditate. Here are a couple:

- *Sit.* Do it for a while. Say half an hour. And don't do anything else. Just relax, and let your mind drift. If you start obsessing about anything, stop and say, "That's quite enough of that!"[21]

- *Be.* This is sort of like "sit," except you're not sitting now, you're doing whatever you happen to be doing. But as you're doing it, you're really paying attention to what you're doing. If you're eating a cookie, for example, take the time to look at it, smell it, and feel it before you stuff it in your mouth. Dissect it, and eat it the way a kid would. Ah, the texture of life is made of moments like this.[22]

❖ **Unwanted thoughts**. Andrew Weil, M.D., has written of the following strategy for managing unwanted thoughts: "putting attention into their opposites. If you are plagued by recurrent, fearful thoughts of getting cancer, think about your immune system constantly weeding out abnormal cells, or when you eat broccoli or drink green tea or take antioxidant supplements, think about how you are strengthening your body's defenses against cancer. Contradictory thoughts will cancel each other out, much as mirror-image sound waves cancel each other out in the new technology of noise elimination."[23]

❖ **Consider trying one of the wide range of comple-mentary therapies**: visualization, diaphragmatic breathing, aromatherapy, biofeedback, hypnotherapy, chiropractics, acupuncture, acupressure.

❖ **Find out what's available for free or low-cost in the community**, such as community college classes, country line dancing, poetry readings, concerts. Good places to look are Departments of Parks and Recreation; community colleges; bookstores; coffee houses; churches; and museums.

❖ **Re-energize**. Have you ever had an instance where you had absolutely no energy, until a friend called and asked you to do something, and suddenly you were energized? This energy is available to be harnessed at other times, too. Triggers are individual, such as play-ing energizing music, planning a reward for the end of the day, or perhaps calling a friend with a last-minute invitation (and energizing both of you).

❖ **Alter the rhythm of your breathing or walking** to calm down (relax) or speed up (energize).

❖ **Find things that both relax AND energize you**. Some ideas to try: green tea, music, nap/sleeping, and exercise.

❖ **A few books to consider**. Your library may have them or be able to get them via interlibrary loan:

- *Earl Mindell's Vitamin Bible* by Earl Mindell

- *Prescription for Nutritional Healing* by James and Phyllis Balch (mental health is covered in the second edition)

- *The Way Up from Down: Rid Yourself of Stress, Low Moods and Depression* by Priscilla Slagle, M.D.

- *Beyond Prozac* by Michael Norden, M.D.

- *Vitamin B-3 & Schizophrenia* by Abram Hoffer, M.D.

❖ **With the pace of change in the Internet world**, recommending websites can be like trying to predict the weather. As of the print date of this book, below are a few of the many excellent websites to consider. Also check out www.procovery.com:

- www.drweil.com is Dr. Andrew Weil's growing site for complementary and herbal medicine, with keyword search capabilities.

- www.mothernature.com has an encyclopedia of natural health with extensive herbal, homeopathic, and drug interaction information.

- www.ncbi.nlm.nih.gov/pubmed allows access to the nine million citations in Medline and other medical research databases free of charge.

- www.mhselfhelp.org is the National Mental Health Consumers' Self-Help Clearinghouse, which also links to www.mentalhelp.net (also known as Mental Health Net), which has extensive mental health self-help resources.

- mental-health-matters.com offers extensive links to self-help and complementary health resources.

- www.iapsrs.org/links.htm from the International Association of Psychosocial Rehabilitation Services also offers extensive links to resources for information on rehabilitation, recovery, mental illness, and advocacy.

❖ **Reward your successes, but choose your rewards**. Use rewards that really *are* rewards, things you will feel better for having done. For example, think about how you will feel afterwards if: after a month of abstaining from alcohol, you celebrate with a bottle of champagne; after a week of dieting, you reward yourself with a big piece of pie; and after a month of successful economizing, you buy something completely out of your budget. Real rewards aren't just pleasurable while we are indulging in them, but feel good afterward, too.

❖ **Go where the energy is.**

When I cannot write a poem, I bake biscuits and feel just as pleased. —Ann Morrow Lindbergh

Procovery Notes for Family

❖ **First and foremost, take care of yourself.**
Otherwise you will be hard pressed to help anyone
else's healing process. I remember telling my daughter
Acasia how there were a few specific people who
would ask for my help when they fell in a pit—but
repeatedly, rather than my succeeding in pulling them
out, they would pull me in. They wouldn't call me
before they were in the pit, only once they were there;
and time and time again I would get pulled in too. She
thoughtfully suggested that, for these particular individuals, I go only close enough to the pit to throw
things in but never close enough to be pulled in.

*"The first rule of holes: when you are in one, stop dig-
ging."* —Molly Ivins

❖ **As many medications will make individuals
crave carbohydrates**, provide healthy "munchies" to
eat together or "to go"—carrots, celery, broccoli, cucum-
ber, cherry tomatoes, unsalted and unbuttered popcorn,
fruit, non-fat yogurt dip.

❖ **Keep a big pitcher of water available**. Water is
helpful for the common side effects of constipation and
dry mouth (and resulting dental havoc) of many psychiatric medications. Maybe add a twist of lemon or
lime, which aids salivation.

❖ **Join a gym or take an exercise class together**. Offer to take a walk or a bike ride.

❖ **Give a stress reducer/sleep enhancer gift (or gift basket)**. For example, I have found these products from Bath & Body Works to be wonderful—Stress Relief linen spray for bedding, Tranquil Sleep bath and shower gel, and Stress Relief mineral bath salts. A couple of other ideas: a soft or pretty or relaxing or happy pillowcase; a night-time mug with a box of "Sleepytime" tea.

❖ **Support self-care actions**. Even if you think they won't help, even if you think it is throwing scarce money away, it may be worth supporting the effort. Trying new things can not only improve one's health but can also increase one's reason to be hopeful, leading to further self-care actions, any one of which could be a turning point toward procovery.

❖ **For substance abuse issues**, seek out information and support from local 12-step support groups for family and friends such as Al-Anon (Alcohol) and Narcotics Anonymous Family Group (Drugs). And for other ideas, see the "Substance Abuse" Procovery Note for Consumers, above.

Procovery Notes for Staff

◈ **Be supportive of individual self-care initiatives,** unless there is a specific therapeutic reason why a self-care strategy would be harmful:

- Individuals diagnosed with a chronic mental illness generally experience a terrifying sense of loss of control over their lives. Self-care initiatives can enhance and restore one's feeling of control over life.

- Often one action leads to another. Ten self-care actions may be taken with no success, but the 11th will be extraordinarily helpful. Support self-care actions so individuals have the stamina and support to make it to the 11th.

◈ **Encourage use of community resources.** Much exists within the community that can help individuals move toward procovery. Whether it is volunteer work, community classes, organized sports, or church, community involvement can be motivating, therapeutic, and cost-effective. Accessing community resources is an excellent and low-cost way to develop highly individualized services that truly meet the goals and interests of the individual.

◈ **A couple of resources to consider**: (1) www.drweil.com is Dr. Andrew Weil's complementary medicine site, which contains good overview information and allows you to pose specific questions; (2) for a source book of clinical research: *Nutritional Influences on Mental Illness* by Dr. Melvyn Werbach.

---

1. Dincin, Jerry (1995). *New Directions, A Pragmatic Approach to Psychiatric Rehabilitation: Lessons from Chicago's Thresholds Program*, 1995 Winter; 68:15. From the standpoint of a personal account of medications being ineffective, see Styron, William. *Darkness Visible*, New York: Random House, p. 54-55.

2. For example, see Carter, C.S., *et. al.* (1995), "Pharmacoeconomics made simple: Risperidone use in a teaching hospital during its first year after market approval, economic and clinical implications," *Psychopharmacology Bulletin*, 31(4):719-725.

3. Shlomo Breznetz, a psychologist at Hebrew University in Jerusalem, "demonstrated that positive and negative expectation have opposite effects on blood levels of cortisol and prolactin, two hormones important in activating the immune system. Breznitz had several groups of Israeli soldiers make a grueling forced march of forty kilometers, but varied the information he gave them. He told some they would march sixty kilometers, but stopped them at forty, and told others they would march thirty kilometers, then said they had another ten to go. Some were allowed to see distance markers, and some had no clues as to how far they had walked or what the total distance would be. Breznitz found that those with the most accurate information weathered the march best, but the stress hormone levels always reflected the soldiers' *estimates* rather than the actual distance." Siegel, Bernie, M.D. (1986). *Love, Medicine and Miracles*, New York: Harper & Row, p. 29.

4. Self-help formats of interventions for alcohol problems can be enhanced by conducting a brief motivational assessment in dispensing the materials. (1966). "A self-help approach for high-risk drinking: Effect of an initial assessment," *Journal of Consulting and Clinical Psychology* 64(4), 694-700.

5. Health Action Network, *DLPA for chronic pain and depression*, San Francisco, 1996.

6. For examples of Amnesty International's concern over sleep deprivation, see their reports 98-09-09, "Five years after the Oslo Agreement: human rights sacrificed for 'security'" (Middle East); 98-05-29, "Long-term prisoners still held under the National Security Law" (South Korea); 98-09-28, "No safe place for prisoners" (Vanautu); 98-04-16, "Confessions extracted under torture—State Injustice: Unfair Trials in the Middle

East and North Africa" (Middle East, 06. Chapter 5); and 98-10-01, "An unfair trial and torture with impunity compromise the establishment of the rule of law" (Mali). Available through the library section of www.amnesty.org.

7. In patients with schizophrenia, there was a reduction in positive symptoms after taking vitamin E. Vitamin E appears to be effective in reducing the severity of tardive dyskinesia, especially in patients who have had TD for five years or less. Lohr, J., Ph.D., and Caligiuri, M., Ph.D. (1996). "Vitamin E Treatment of Tardive Dyskinesia." *Journal of Clinical Psychiatry* 1996;57:167-173.

8. Hoffer, Abram, M.D. (1998). *Vitamin B-3 & Schizophrenia*, Ontario, Canada: Quarry Press, www.quarrypress.com.

9. Mindell, Earl (1991). *Earl Mindell's Vitamin Bible*, New York: Warner Books, p. 33.

10. Weil, Andrew, M.D. (1995). "Relieving Depression Simply," *Dr. Andrew Weil's Self Healing Newsletter*, 1(1):8. Publisher Watertown MA:Thorne Communications, 617-926-0200.

11. *Id.*

12. Norden, Michael (1995). *Beyond Prozac*, New York: Harper Collins, p. 68-69.

13. Balch, James, M.D., and Balch, Phyllis, C.N.C. (1997). *Prescription for Nutritional Healing*, Garden City Park, New York: Avery Publishing, p. 107, 241. *Also see* Werbach, Melvyn, M.D. (1991). *Nutritional Influences on Mental Illness*, Tarzana, California: Third Line Press, p. 18.

14. Weil, Andrew, M.D., www.drweil.com, "Ask Dr. Weil" database (search keyword "constipation," specific page is located at www.pathfinder.com/drweil/database/display/0,1412,33,00.html.

15. Mindell, Earl (1991). *Earl Mindell's Vitamin Bible*, New York: Warner Books, p. 166-167.

16. Balch, James, M.D., and Balch, Phyllis, C.N.C. (1997). *Prescription for Nutritional Healing*, Garden City Park, New York: Avery Publishing, p. 212.

17. Weil, Andrew, M.D., www.drweil.com, "Ask Dr. Weil" database (search keyword "dry mouth," specific page is "Q&A: Seeking a solution for dry mouth?") www.pathfinder.com/drweil/archiveqa/0,2283,1572,00.html.

18. Simple Living Network, *101 Ways To Slow Things Down*, www.slnet.com/free/newsletter/19articles/10ways.htm.

19. *Id.*

20. Balch, James, M.D., and Balch, Phyllis, C.N.C. (1997). *Prescription for Nutritional Healing*, Garden City Park, New York: Avery Publishing, p. 498.

21. Simple Living Network, *101 Ways To Slow Things Down*, www.slnet.com/free/ newsletter/19articles/10ways.htm.

22. *Id.*

23. Weil, Andrew, M.D. (1995). *Spontaneous Healing*, New York: Knopf, p. 198.

Living Intentionally Through Work and Activities

Let us stop equating work with earning a living, but rather think of it as an important component of making a life. —Ralph C. Weinrich

Diagnosis may be specific, but healing is holistic—involving medical, psychological, legal, familial, spiritual, and financial components—any one of which, properly aided, can make the defining difference in procovery. Work and meaningful activities are integral to many of these components.

One's choice of work and activities can be reactive or intentional. *Reactive* choices respond to the daily pressures of life; this is the manner in which many people operate regularly, and can be difficult to avoid for individuals who must also cope with the daily struggles of chronic illness. *Intentional* choices, in the context of procovery, are those made with specific questions in mind, including: Will it help me procover? Is it the best use of my time? What are the pluses and minuses?

Recognizing Choices

For the secret of man's being is not only to live but to have something to live for. —Fyodor Dostoyevsky

Most simply stated, what we do all day matters. Any time spent doing one thing is time not spent doing another. Spending time in a way that will best move one toward procovery is critical.

Activities pursued, whether educational or recreational, work-related or spiritual, should be considered on the basis of how they will affect one's procovery in the long view.

For example, for one person, watching television every evening—done after full days of work, school, etc.—might be a relaxing, fun, unstructured time that helps transition to a good night's sleeping. For another, it could be a tool to kill time where little is gained and opportunity is lost. It can be helpful to consider activities by asking whether in the long view—in a week, a month, or a year—it would be the best use of your time in moving toward procovery.

The Role of Activities in Procovery

Life is what happens when you're busy doing other things. —John Lennon

The way you spend your time, the activities you choose, can be a primary way to be both productive and fulfilled; they can be a primary catalyst for healing, a reason and a way to move forward.

It's easy, however, for individuals to fall into the trap of waiting for some future time to involve themselves in life, in ways they find meaningful. At such times individuals, with ample justification, reason that "I'm too sick now," or "I can hardly get through the day as it is," or "so little is available to me," or "I can't do the things I used to love doing, why bother?" or "I have nothing to offer," or "I haven't decided what I want to do yet."

Although clearly there are times when just getting through the day is heroic, habits can develop that become self-limiting and self-defeating. Do you feel—

- Isolated and lonely?

- Trapped?

- That the magic is gone from life, that there are very few positive surprises left?

- That you have little to look forward to, that your days are remarkably similar and run into each other?

- That fewer options are now available to you?

- That your world feels smaller (and not in a good way) than it once was?

It can be life-changing to get connected to others, to interests you are passionate about (or become passionate about over time). It is important to try new things, and to measure whether they are procovery-building. Ask yourself—before, during, or after an activity:

- Do you find you are more energetic?

- More interested in life?

- More inspired?

- More hopeful?

- Waking up to other new ideas and possibilities?

- Are you growing?

- Do you feel life has more meaning?

Procovery-oriented activities differ person to person. Decide where to start, what to try. Ask yourself: What did I used to like to do? Is any of it still available to me now? What did I dream before I stopped dreaming? What would make me want to get out of bed in the morning? What do I get goose bumps or tingle just thinking about doing?

If nothing gives you goose bumps (yet!), and you don't know where to begin, consider what is easily available to try. Ask others if they have any activities they might recommend, keeping your personality, interests, and goals in mind. Or ask someone whose company you enjoy whether they might take a class with you.

Gather as many ideas as possible. Look at your list and ask yourself about each idea: What do I gain? What do I lose? Will it likely enable me to express myself and to grow and procover?

It is essential not to confuse the *idea* with the *fit*. As in, "I thought a support group would be a good idea but it wasn't."

Many times it is just a matter of finding the right fit for you. You may find one volunteer job degrading and another inspiring. You may find one support group unsupportive and another a life-line. You may find one potential living situation or drop-in center an energy-sucking environment and another energizing.

Don't wait to become involved in life until you are fully procovered. Becoming involved *is* procovering!

Pursuit **is** *happiness.* —Ernest Hemingway

The Role of Work in Procovery

Although people need help to deal with their emotional problems, if they don't have some way to make a living, they will never truly be able to enter, or re-enter, the mainstream. —Joseph Rogers[1]

The importance of work is rooted deeply in us. As Matthew Fox writes in *The Reinvention of Work*, "We prepare ourselves for work by getting an education; we work; we recover from work; and we try to raise children who can successfully enter the work world." Erich Fromm describes in *The Sane Society* the deeper basis of work:

> "Work is not only an inescapable necessity for man. Work is also his liberator from nature, his creator as a social and independent being. *In the process of work, that is, the molding and changing of nature outside of himself, man molds and changes himself.*

Bookstore shelves are brimming with titles about *meaningful* work, but the reality is that work for most people is at best a mixed bag. Studs Terkel writes in *Working* that "[w]ork by its very nature, [is] about violence—to the spirit as well as to the body. It is about ulcers as well as accidents, about shouting matches as well as fist-fights, about nervous breakdowns as well as kicking the dog around. It is, above all (or beneath all), about daily humiliations. To survive the day is triumph enough for the walking wounded among the great many of us."

For many individuals diagnosed with psychiatric disorders, this mixed bag gets worse:

> . . . And of course you've lost your job. Who could work amid all this drug experimentation? And the myriad of drug side effects—nausea, diarrhea, dizziness. Vision so bad you can't cross the street because you cannot judge the cars' distance from you. Drug-induced psychosis so bad you can't leave your bed or look out the window for the terror you feel. Blood pressure so low you can't stand for very long, and your voice so weak you can't be heard across a telephone wire.

> So, you're without a job. And they send you to a place called DVR—Division of Vocational Rehabilitation. They 'help' you get a clerical job. Never mind that you don't want to do that kind of work. Never mind that you have a degree—or two. They 'help' you get a clerical job because, yes, you have guessed it, you're a CMI [Chronically Mentally Ill]. A woman CMI. But the men CMIs are just as lucky. They get to become janitors.
> —Betty Blaska, M.A.[2]

This leads to the basic question facing many individuals diagnosed with mental illness: Are the risks of working worth the rewards? Or, more briefly, why work?

The overtones of this question—philosophical, moral, political, spiritual, lifestyle—are beyond the scope of this book. What is not beyond the scope of this book is the question, when might work contribute to an individual's procovery? And in that regard, the following questions are offered to help individuals identify whether work may significantly contribute to their procovery, particularly in the long view:

- Will I feel better about myself if I'm working? More pride, more hope, more needed, more contributing, more "autonomous"?

- Will work be a better use of my time than what I am currently doing?

- Will I have more money, if not immediately then down the road?

- How will it improve or affect my medical coverage or other benefits?

- Will the structure and routine required by a job help me procover?

- Will working help me focus more on life rather than on illness?

- Will work likely serve as a positive reminder of how far I've come?

- Will working increase my contact with others with whom I might become friends, date, or network for other employment opportunities?

- Will a job provide me with growth opportunities, professional and otherwise?

- Will this job help me build my work history? (Just as it is often difficult to get credit before you have credit, it can be difficult getting a job you want because of a lack of related work history.)

- Will I still be able to do what I need from a health standpoint to procover?

The answers to these questions will often indicate that— even if one is starting out at an entry level (where even individuals with degrees and strong work histories may find themselves), risking benefits, possibly only breaking even financially, and significantly increasing stress—work can be a central factor in promoting procovery.

Work Strategies

Many of us are jobless, not because we are not capable of working, but because we are taught that we are unemployable. —Ed Irwin

Despite serious and numerous systemic disincentives, many individuals find work to be an important element in healing.[3] Given these disincentives, and the difficulties of coping with a chronic illness (let alone *working* with one) what strategies will help?

Building up gradually: There is significant opportunity for individuals in the enormous gray zone between being unemployed and full-time, paid employment. Many individuals, for health reasons and/or concerns over risking government or other benefits, may find it best to explore incremental, gradual steps forward. Volunteering and part-time work can be excellent steps to consider, and often can result in a helpful reference—and full-time paid employment if and when desired.

Looking for work: Some personnel experts will say there are only three proven job-hunting strategies—networking, networking, and networking—but there are other methods, including newspaper ads, searching online, and permanent and temp employment agencies. And there are innumerable ways to network, including asking friends and relatives about jobs where they work, and requesting "informational" meetings with professionals in the firms or fields in which you are interested. You might begin by trying as many different search methods as you can think of, but over time focus your energy on those that seem to get the best results.

Simply avoiding common interviewing mistakes will dramatically improve your chances of being hired. Be on time; pay attention to your appearance—it is often suggested to dress for the job you want rather than the job you have or are interviewing for. Ask questions *and listen*; be prepared ahead of time to answer the question as to why you are an excellent candidate. Answer the dreaded "what are your weaknesses" question with weaknesses that won't harm your ability to do your job (you don't get enough exercise) or the employer will like (you work too much) or you can fix (you don't know their spreadsheet software but you are a quick learner). Be the only candidate who actually asks for and reads the company's annual report and marketing literature *before* the interview.

Choosing work pace: The best work pace will vary with the individual. "One consumer gave up lucrative working in the area of his training for a low paid maintenance job because the former work pace, fast and demanding, led to symptoms of his illness. Another consumer, in spite of multiple crises and one hospitalization, claimed rehabilitation and strength through the rigorous, fast-paced schedule her job required."[4]

Selective disclosure of diagnosis to co-workers and employers: The decision "to tell or not to tell" has practical and psychological layers, both in interviewing and in working on the job. The simple fact is that individuals are not defined by their illness *unless they so define themselves*. (Legally, under the 1990 Americans with Disabilities Act, an employer cannot ask a job applicant whether he or she has a disability or needs a reasonable accommodation.)

Legal rights: The 1990 Americans with Disabilities Act (ADA) gives individuals with psychiatric disabilities protection against discrimination in the workplace and under certain circumstances requires employers to make "reasonable accommodations" for disabled workers. The Bazelon Center for Mental Health Law has a guide as to how the ADA applies to individuals with psychiatric disabilities at www.bazelon.org/eeocguid.html. The Center for Psychiatric Rehabilitation at Boston University offers practical guidance on what the ADA requires and how individuals might approach disclosing disabilities to employers and schools, at www.bu.edu/sarpsych/jobschool. If you believe an employer has violated this law, contact the local office of the U.S. Equal Employment Opportunity Commission (the national number is 202-663-4264).[5]

Another issue on the job that can affect employees diagnosed with psychiatric disorders is drug testing. Testing is particularly prevalent in public safety, transportation, mining, construction, and national security (large firms are more likely to test than small firms).[6] Stephen Isaacs, J.D., writes, "Generally, job applicants have no right to object to a drug test. You can, of course refuse to take one, but if you do, the employer has no obligation to hire you. Employees have more grounds to contest a company's drug-testing policy . . . under the state constitution or laws."[7] This is a complex and developing area of the law; you might contact the local affiliate or chapter of the American Civil Liberties Union (the headquarters is in

New York, 212-549-2900; the Web site www.aclu.org has a good "briefing paper" overview of the law).

Using a mentor: It is helpful to have a one-on-one "get and keep a job" support person, similar to having your own personal coach. This mentor could be a family member, friend, social worker, etc. He or she could help you draft a resume; analyze options; look into training possibilities; serve as a reference, select clothes to wear for interviews and jobs; sift through the impact work might have on any government or other benefits; and make a dry run of the transportation required if it is unfamiliar to you.

Maintaining work: Early on, keeping a job can be as tough as getting one. Often people find themselves initially exhausted, pressed for time, and have difficulty transitioning from work to home to sleep to work. Strategies that can help include:

- Setting priorities ("In the morning I get things done, make my calls. I start with whatever bothers me the most.")[8]

- Planning ahead for absence, e.g., saving up vacation, personal time, and sick days for mental health leave; finding a confidant among co-workers or supervisors who can cover for such an absence.[9]

- A written reminder as to why you chose to work, for those times you question the decision.

- Developing and allowing time for a morning routine, e.g., taking a brisk walk, listening to Mozart and having a cup of green tea, doing a crossword puzzle, meeting a co-worker for coffee.

- Allowing for unwinding time before bed—warm milk, Sleepytime tea, a jigsaw puzzle, playing a game of cards, playing relaxing music, or doing relaxation breathing.

- Many find, upon beginning or initially returning to work, a need for an extraordinary amount of sleep. Allow for this!

- Laying clothes out the night or weekend before.

- Setting up "work dates" with friends to stay in touch and still get errands done, e.g., a washing night at the laundromat, going grocery shopping and grabbing a cup of coffee, cooking together a stew and lasagna over the weekend to split for weekday meals.

A mentor can help with many of these strategies, allowing you to vent and to help brainstorm coping strategies or solutions, and also reminding you when you're frustrated how work fits into your bigger picture and why you've chosen it. As Willis Harman has said, "What is really important is not so much what work a person does, but what he perceives he is doing it for."

In or Out of the Mental Health Arena?

Everyone has been made for some particular work, and the desire for that work has been put in every heart. —Rumi

Some individuals find it validating to work in mental health, and a good way to use their expertise both to help others and to build marketable skills. Others find it hard to move forward when their work or activities are focused in the mental health area, constantly reminding them of their own experiences.

As William Anthony, Ph.D., notes, "One need not have a specific credential to practice psychiatric rehabilitation. Rather, one must be interpersonally skilled and be able to set goals with consumers, assess and teach skills, negotiate with the consumers' support system. . . . Consumers themselves can become excellent practitioners of psychiatric rehabilitation."[10]

The challenge for procovering individuals, and those who work with them, is to accept that either choice can be valid, and that an individual's choice can change over time.

Living Intentionally

The cost of a thing is the amount of what I call life which is required to be exchanged for it, immediately or in the long run. —Henry David Thoreau

How to earn a living while making a life can be a dilemma for anyone. Procovering individuals have the added consideration of earning a living in a manner that will support their procovery.

Living with chronic illness is demanding. One's natural reserves for life's stresses are depleted by the daily stressors associated with chronic illness.

That may mean choosing a job with less financial return but with flexibility such as job sharing, reduced hours, and frequent breaks. If a compromise needs to be made in choosing between money and procovery, it is important to choose procovery if at all possible—otherwise neither may be gained.

Money will buy a pretty good dog, but it will not buy the wag of its tail. —Josh Billings

The very reason that living intentionally is so important for procovering individuals is also the reason such individuals are often among those best equipped to do so with wisdom and perspective. Those who, to use Albert Schweitzer's phrase, are of the "fellowship of those who bear the mark of pain" have a depth of experience and insight as to what matters in the long run, what is important in life and, perhaps more essential, what isn't.

Procovery Notes for Consumers

❖ **Don't confuse the value of work with the pay scale or "level" of the work.** All that matters is how *you* value the job. Does it further your procovery, making you healthier rather than sicker? Stay away from jobs where you cannot build your feelings of self-efficacy.

The society which scorns excellence in plumbing because plumbing is a humble activity, and tolerates shoddiness in philosophy because philosophy is an exalted activity, will have neither good plumbing nor good philosophy. Neither its pipes nor its theories will hold water. —John W. Gardner

❖ **Consumer drop-in centers, day programs, etc. should choose activities intentionally** and on the basis of procovery impact. Possibilities include a stigmabusting theater group; yoga classes; fund-raisers for day and weekend trips; workshops on money management, resume writing, advocacy, organization/simplification, keeping a journal, how to communicate and express anger, self-care, how to start a support group, local educational opportunities, job fairs, and how to collaborate with health care professionals.

❖ **Consider temping.** Be clear with a temp agency about how many hours a month you can commit to work based on your overall health, availability, and benefits limitations.

Temping can lead to a full-time job. Les Krantz writes in *Job Finder's Guide*, "If you need to boost your credentials in a particular field, consider seeking assignments that provide training and expertise in that area. Tell your temporary agency representative that training is your top priority in accepting assignments."

Go where your energy is—perhaps by attending or teaching a class on spirituality; starting a support group; offering to write movie or book reviews for your local paper or community or support group; or going for a degree program in a field that really matters to you.

❖ **If you are interested in a college and/or a graduate degree**, it may be worth checking into the growing range of accredited degrees available by distance learning through home study and the Internet. Many of these programs indicate that they offer credit for life experience. (Thomas Edison State College in Trenton, New Jersey, 888-442-TESC, offers a free "Portfolio Assessment Handbook.") Take a look at "Bear's Guide to Earning Degrees Nontraditionally" by John Bear (Degree.net Books, El Cerrito, California) or do a search on any Web search engine for "distance learning" or "distance degrees."

❖ **Get in touch with your natural abilities.** People tend to value what comes difficult to them and devalue what comes easily.

❖ **When asked your strengths, keep in mind all you have to offer that is marketable**, e.g., are you punctual, friendly, an eager or quick learner, a people person, detail oriented, good under pressure; do you have proofreading or editing skills, take direction easily?

❖ **Be prepared to answer a standard interview question**, "What are your weaknesses?" You might offer something that the employer already knows but flip it into a strength, such as, "I don't have past experience, but I am very interested and quick to learn," or, "Although I prefer to start a little later in the morning if possible, I am happy to stay late," "I have no work references at this point, but I have several excellent personal references that I would be pleased to provide."

❖ **Ask about the job and/or company**. AND LISTEN!

No man ever listened himself out of a job.
—Calvin Coolidge

❖ **It is often not the person with the most experience or credentials who secures a position**, but the person who interviews the best. Sometimes you can make up in enthusiasm for a deficit in another area.

❖ **There are exceptions to most job-hunting rules**. When people are looking for work, they often don't do things because "that's not the way it's done." In fact, many jobs are found by breaking the rules, combining your skills and interests with an unusual contact or approach.

◈ **Consider job fairs**. Employers with job openings often gather in one place. One place to check for job fairs is your local Sunday newspaper classified listings.

◈ **A variety of internships and apprenticeships, paid and volunteer, exist on an international basis**. There are a large number of internship directories on the web—start with www.infoseek.com or www.yahoo.com and enter "internship" as the search term.

◈ **Volunteer positions can lead to paid positions**, can be useful for resume and reference purposes, and can be a good way to test the waters.

◈ **Take a temporary seasonal job and excel at it**. It will add to your resume, and some holiday temps are retained as permanent employees.

◈ **Creating a resume and cover letter**. If you do have a good chronological job history oriented toward the type of job you want, a chronological resume is the traditional and often preferred approach. If not, consider a "functional" resume, that doesn't emphasize timelines or job titles, but rather highlights your skills, talents, and accomplishments, grouping them within functional areas or according to your overall job goals and objectives. Often you can set yourself apart from your competition simply by having a brief, well-crafted, and error-free cover letter.

◈ **At the close of an interview, consider asking, "Do I have the job?"** or "What can I do to get this job?" or "When will I hear if I have the job?"

◈ **References**. When asked for references, supply those a prospective employer is likely to most value, i.e., a reference who is likely to say what the employer wants to hear in a way the employer can identify with—e.g., conscientious, detail-oriented, reliable, team player, etc.

Offer references not of those individuals who like you the most, but those individuals who will give the most professional, work-related reference. Rather than hearing that you are the "nicest guy in the world," employers will likely want to hear that you are "dedicated," "a quick learner," "do what it takes to get the job done," "a computer whiz", etc. It can be helpful to let your references know ahead of time the nature of the job you are seeking, so that they can tailor the reference to the job.

◈ **Be sure to leave prospective employers a phone number at which you can be easily reached** (preferably with an answering machine with a professional-sounding outgoing message). If this can't be done, ask when you might call the employer.

⬦ **Choosing between jobs.** As every job has pluses and minuses, it can be useful to prioritize your individual preferences, perhaps taking into consideration the following questions:

- What is the job's economic impact (compensation vs. costs of child care, clothing, meals, transportation)?

- What is the job's likely therapeutic impact?

- What is the difficulty or ease of commuting?

- What is the impact on benefits (medical coverage, disability)?

- Does the job offer training you want?

- Is there opportunity for advancement?

- How interesting or exciting is the job?

⬦ **Untangling the impact of working on benefits.** Some individuals diagnosed with psychiatric disorders receive government disability benefits, including Social Security Disability Insurance (SSDI), Supplemental Security Income (SSI), and Medicare. The general guideline for disability benefits is a physical or mental impairment that prevents you from doing any substantially gainful work. The following contacts may be helpful in sorting out this issue:

- U.S. Social Security Administration, 800-772-1213 (mainly helpful for getting forms)

- Your local state Protection and Advocacy group (to find yours, contact the National Association of Protection and Advocacy Systems at 202-408-9514 or www.protectionandadvocacy.com)

- Bazelon Center for Mental Health Law, 202-467-5730 or www.bazelon.org

- National Organization of Social Security Claimants' Representatives (provides referrals to attorneys specializing in Social Security cases, but note that any attorney can get on the list so it does not guarantee expertise), 800-431-2804

- Boston University Law School, N. Neal Pike Institute on Law and Disability, www.bu.edu/pike/home.html

- U.S. Department of Justice Americans with Disabilities Act home page, www.usdoj.gov/crt/ada/adahom1.htm

◈ **Thrift stores can be an excellent source of work attire**. In addition, consider holding or attending a clothing swap or sale at your home, church, support group, etc.

Procovery Notes for Family Members

◈ **Job-hunting assistance**. You might help research prospective employers; sort through benefits language, etc.; get letters of reference (perhaps a family friend, neighbor, etc.); assess natural strengths and abilities as well as traditional skills; help put together a work wardrobe.

◈ **Job survival assistance**. Listen to frustrations; discuss possible ideas for "small talk" to explore common ground with co-workers; offer reminders of past successes and accomplishments when frustration is building; to the extent you have time available you might help with transportation or errands.

◈ **Offer to take a workshop or class together**; volunteer for a mutually interesting organization such as a local food pantry; or join a speaking group such as Toastmasters International (to find a local Toastmasters club, see www.toastmasters.org, or contact them at P.O. Box 9052, Mission Viejo, CA 92690, 949-858-8255).

◈ **Help locate growth opportunities through volunteering, apprenticeships, and internships.**

◈ **Together adopt even the tiniest neglected public plot of dirt to plant flowers,** create a rock garden or otherwise tend. Often senior citizen centers would tremendously appreciate assistance with window boxes and/or gardening.

⬧ **Food matters**. A favorite casserole, fresh muffins, or favorite cookies can seem like small favors—but they not only save money and time, they send a message of love.

Procovery Notes for Staff

⬧ **Don't confuse the value of work with the pay scale or "level" of the work**. What matters is how individuals value their job. Does it further their pro-covery, making them healthier rather than sicker? Jobs that do not build self-efficacy are unlikely to move someone toward procovery.

⬧ **Discuss possible helpful changes in medication**, e.g., if early rising is desired or required, taking med-ication earlier in the evening.

⬧ **Make sure an emergency number (perhaps a 24-hour hot-line) is available**, as returning or adjust-ing to work, although generally beneficial, can increase stress early on.

⬧ **Be careful not to attribute all job difficulties to illness**. All individuals experience work-related difficulties and stress.

❖ **Help individuals where possible with daily work issues**—such as "interpreting the behaviors of co-workers (for example, whether a particular statement was playful or threatening), understanding how personal their work relationships should be (for example, whether to ask co-workers if they are married or whether to give a supervisor a get-well card), and recognizing how their own behaviors affect others (for example, that withdrawn or overexcited behavior might be off-putting)."[11]

❖ **Someone job-switching three or four times in a year** might be considered flitzy, unfocused, "not ready" for work, when in fact just the opposite is true; the individual is effectively exploring alternatives.

"My bouncing from job to job sent a message to my counselors and—as a result of their attitudes—to me that I wasn't ready for work. But it is not uncommon for people to bounce from job to job. Sometimes this is in the spirit of adventure; or someone might take a job that is wrong for them, so they look for another. This behavior is normal for people investigating the job market for the first time. It is one of the ways you discover what you want to do, and it is considered acceptable behavior—for most of the population, that is. But I had a psychiatric history, and I was given to understand that if I was lucky enough to find a job, I damn well better hold onto it—because leaving the job would constitute failure. . . . A work-study program where

people can spend three months or six months trying
out a variety of occupations seems like an effective
model."[12]

1. Rogers, J.A. (1995). "Work is key to recovery," *Psychosocial Rehabilitation Journal*,
18(4):5-10.

2. Blaska, Betty, M.A. (1995). "What it is like to be treated as a CMI," *The Mental
Health System: Consumer Survival Guide, Notes From People Who Have Been There*,
Wisconsin Statewide Consumer/Survivor Network, August 1995, p. 41.

3. "All consumers in this study described employment as an important means of coping
with severe mental illness." Alverson, M., Becker, D., and Drake, R. (1995). "An ethnographic study of coping strategies used by people with severe mental illness participating in supported employment," *Psychosocial Rehabilitation Journal*, 18(4):115-128.

4. *Id.*

5. EEOC enforcement guidance on the ADA, EEOC Notice Number 915.002 Date 3-25-97,
as of the date of the publication of this book, is on the Web at www.eeoc.gov/docs/psych.
txt.

6. Hartwell, Steele, French, and Rodman (1996). "Prevalence of drug testing in the
workplace," *Monthly Labor Review*, November 1996, p. 35-42

7. Isaacs, Stephen, and Swartz, Ava (1992). *The Consumer's Legal Guide to Today's
Health Care*, New York: Houghton Mifflin Company, p. 103. This excellent resource
offers practical legal advice about a wide range of health care issues.

8. Alverson, M., Becker, D., and Drake, R. (1995). "An ethnographic study of coping
strategies used by people with severe mental illness participating in supported employment," *Psychosocial Rehabilitation Journal*, 18(4):115-128.

9. *Id.*

10. Anthony, W.A. (1996). "Integrating psychiatric rehabilitation into managed care,"
Psychiatric Rehabilitation Journal, 20(2): 39-44.

11. Lysaker, P., Bell, M., Milstein, R., Bryson, G., Shestopal, A., and Goulet, J.B. (1993).
"Work capacity in Schizophrenia," *Hospital and Community Psychiatry*, 44(3): 278-280.

12. Rogers, J.A. (1995). "Work is key to recovery," *Psychosocial Rehabilitation Journal*,
18(4):5-10.

Special Considerations

This book is intended to be an overview of procovery—individual procovery approaches for specific populations are beyond its scope.

However, because the procovery potential for children and elderly individuals diagnosed with emotional and psychiatric disorders is so often misunderstood, it is important to emphasize that the concepts and strategies of procovery offer hope and healing equally to these individuals.

Toward that end, the sections below briefly highlight some of the key aspects of procovery for both children and elderly individuals diagnosed with psychiatric disorders.

Procovery and the Elderly

Elderly individuals procover the same way others do, focusing on strengths rather than weaknesses, on personal preferences and on what is available, asking, "What can I do, with what I have, now?"

What does procovery look like for elderly individuals with psychiatric diagnoses? A life deemed worth living, despite illness and/or hardships that are faced. This is a completely personal measure—it may be pride in choosing an outfit even if one can no longer dress oneself, or having lunch out with friends occasionally even if one cannot cook dinner, or singing in church on Sunday even if one can no longer be a member of the church choir.

Procovery is defined as "attaining a productive and fulfilling life regardless of the level of health assumed attainable." But what does "productive" mean? As a society we tend to measure whether we are *externally* productive, whether we create, for example, wealth or material goods. But—and perhaps particularly with regard to elderly individuals—it is essential to seek and value being *internally* productive. Erich Fromm, in referring to "inner activity" as the "productive use of our human powers,"[1] recognized that knowledge, insight, and feelings can be among the highest results of productivity. Such results are well within the scope of most elderly individuals, whose experience and wisdom far outweigh any physical limitations of age and disability.

A few procovery strategies to consider:

Don't attribute every symptom to age. Michael McGarvey, M.D., tells a story about a 92 year-old man who visited his doctor complaining of pain in his right knee. "With your age," said the doctor, "what do you expect?" "I don't know," said the man. "My left knee is also 92, but it feels great. So you tell me, what should I expect?"

Physical and mental illnesses must be managed together, particularly given the multiple illnesses and symptoms often confronting the elderly. As geriatric psychiatrist William Flynn, M.D., notes, "There is no substitute for psychiatrists and primary care physicians to work collaboratively."

Elderly individuals and their caregivers need special attention and education focused on medication management. Fine tuning regarding medication choices, dosage, and timing is critical. Elderly individuals often have multiple doctors prescribing multiple medications for multiple physical and mental ailments. At the same time, elderly individuals often receive medications with little understanding of their purpose, dosage, and side effects, or the possible interactions with over-the-counter drugs.

Don't only treat illness and symptoms; develop shared goals to enhance life. We all need a reason to get out of bed, something to look forward to, and it is those goals that generally drive our motivation to seek and comply with treatment, as well as our ability to heal. Feeling visible, needed, loved, connected is often more desired than symptom reduction. As Lee Jones, M.D., has stated, "Don't assume what most matters to someone is in their list of symptoms." Geriatric psychiatrist William Flynn, M.D., cites everyday examples of potential individual goals:

• I want to live in a more home-like setting.

• I want to have a friend.

• I want to be able to go sing at church on Sunday.

- I want to not always have to be on the oxygen tank—now that I am oxygen-dependent I am never able to go on outings; I would like to somehow go out to lunch like I used to.

- I'd like to go to a movie occasionally.

- I'd like to have my own apartment.

Remember that as individuals age, they don't lose the desire to feel needed, or loved, or touched. Soliciting their advice, learning from their experience, hugging them, offering a back or foot rub—ordinary things we all love—are as essential to procovery as the right balance of medications or any other treatment offered.

Forget how old you are and keep on planning—just as though you're going to keep on living. The one thing that keeps you going is to have an objective. You should have ambitions, and work to fulfill them. Then you can forget those actuary tables and life expectancy statistics."
—Rodney Jones, at the age of 101

Procovery and Children

I learned what every dreaming child needs to know—that no horizon is so far you cannot get above it or beyond it . . .
—Beryl Markham

We want so much to protect children from harm—to see them grow and shine. The very idea of a diagnosis of serious emotional disturbance[2] can be heartbreaking. Moving children forward to procovery requires remembering that they can still grow and shine and enjoy all of the possibility and beauty in life. A diagnosis of an emotional disorder is just one small aspect of a child.

> . . . I told her that nothing I'd written was specific to ADD [attention deficit disorder], but any of my books would deal with the issue in general terms.
>
> 'No,' she said, 'that won't do. I need something specific.'
>
> 'Why?' I asked, curious regarding her urgency.
>
> 'Because my eight-year-old son *is* ADD,' she answered (emphasis hers).
>
> Oh, my. This woman thinks her son is, in his entirety, in every fiber of his being, in every aspect of who he is and can ever hope to become, ADD. He is nothing more and nothing less than ADD. He is no longer simply a child. He has become a category, a subset of child. He is a prefix. He is ADD.
>
> This woman, like so many American parents of her generation, has gone to a professional who has rendered this diagnosis concerning her son. I am not questioning the diagnosis. I might have suggested this myself. But I would have told the woman this: 'Do not be misled by this diagnosis, this condition we're going to call attention deficit disorder. It constitutes perhaps 10 percent of your son's overall makeup. The other 90

percent of him is just like every other eight-year-old in the world. If you forget that, you do so at his, and your, peril. —Dr. John Rosemond

A few procovery strategies to consider:

Don't over-symptomize. Once a diagnosis is made, it can be easy to read into it all kinds of natural, healthy behavior as being a sign of illness rather than a sign of childhood.

Make it clear to a child that the diagnosis is not the result of a choice or a personal flaw. That he or she is not any more "different" than anyone else; that we all have a huge degree of commonality as well as other aspects that set us apart; that these differences make the world go around; that everyone has strengths and weaknesses; and that you are proud of him or her and see great things in his or her future.

My husband once asked me how it was possible that I evolved unscathed from my upbringing with a mentally ill brother. It never occurred to me that as a family we should have fallen apart. To me my brother's illness was just a fact. Like Daddy went to work on Monday mornings. It was O.K. for him to be that way, and it was O.K. for us to be happy. It was simple—you love your family, you care for each individual, you respect each other. It always felt solid, it felt right.
—D. Marsh and R. Dickens[3]

There is not one answer to procovery; procovery is generally reached by an accumulation of helpful things that ultimately snowball into procovery. Try to design a base plan that might include:

- Medication

- Relaxation techniques

- Structure and/or routine: i.e., sleeping, eating, bath time, etc.

- Transition time/scheduled time for both unwinding and revving up

Don't compare children, either child to child, or the same child pre- and post-diagnosis. As John Holt writes about education, "The child wants to grow, to step forward, to move out into the world. But he has to move from where he is. If we can't or won't reach him where he is, we can't encourage or help him make those next steps. Instead, we freeze him into immobility."

Facilitate communication and healthy expression of feelings. Help children explore how best (or whether to) relate any information about their diagnosis to others, as well as how to express their wide range of feelings in a healthy manner, and how to monitor their self talk. (Often we say negative things to ourselves we would never allow others to say.)

Find at least one thing to do every day just for fun—with no measured outcome. Don't let daily life become pressured, routine, and monotonous. Make sure you make time for the magic of childhood!

Know you what it is to be a child?

It is to be something very different

from the man of today.

It is to have a spirit yet streaming

from the waters of baptism;

it is to believe in love,

to believe in loveliness,

to believe in belief;

it is to be so little

that the elves can reach to whisper in your ear;

it is to turn pumpkins into coaches,

and mice into horses,

lowness into loftiness,

and nothing into everything,

for each child has

its fairy godmother in its soul.

—Francis Thompson Shelley

1. Fromm, Erich (1976). *To Have or To Be?* New York: Bantam, p. 76.

2. "Serious Emotional Disturbance" (SED) is a term that covers a broad range of behavioral, mental, and emotional disorders, including attention deficit disorder (with or without hyperactivity), conduct disorder, depression, anxiety disorders, eating disorders (anorexia nervosa, bulimia, etc.), schizophrenia, pervasive developmental disorder, Tourette's syndrome, and others. It does not include mental retardation, autism, or other developmental disabilities such as epilepsy or cerebral palsy. (Source: "Children With Serious Emotional Disturbance: Troubled and Troubling Children," National Mental Health Association, Fact Sheet, August 1997.)

3. Marsh, D.T., & Dickens, R.M. (1997). *Troubled journey: Coming to terms with the mental illness of a sibling or parent*, New York: Tarcher/Putnam.

Retaining Procovery: The Benefit of the Bargain

We must be willing to get rid of the life we've planned so as to have the life that is waiting for us. —Joseph Campbell

Chronic illness comes at a tremendous cost. Emotional and physical pain and suffering, money, time, innocence, dreams.

But do individuals gain anything from illness? Having procovered from chronic mental illness, are we richer?

The Benefit of the Procovery Bargain

People who have not been in Narnia sometimes think that a thing cannot be good and terrible at the same time. —C.S. Lewis

Henry David Thoreau wrote in *Walden* that "the mass of men lead lives of quiet desperation." It strikes me that this quiet desperation often stems from a lack of purpose or meaning. Illness can be an initiator, a spark, a catalyst that leads one to search and find the meaning to drive not only one's healing but one's life.

As Viktor Frankl wrote in *Man's Search for Meaning*, "once an individual's search for meaning is successful, it not only renders him happy but also gives him the capability to cope with suffering."

On the path to procovery, individuals use the extreme hardship of chronic illness to find and become not who they were but who they can be now. Simply put, having earned a rebirth through procovery, one's life holds more meaning as a result of illness, not less.

We as Americans have an unhealthy definition of health. We think it means the elimination of all pain and the eradication of all disease. Rather, it means living a life well. —Russell D. Pierce, J.D.

Health is aliveness, spontaneity, gracefulness, and rhythm —Alexander Lowen, M.D.

The meaning and insight that can result from procovery include:

What is important in life and what isn't. In the face of losing so much, what is important can leap into focus more loud and clear than ever, and that lesson should never be lost.

What your body requires. You are the world's greatest authority on you. In the process of procovery, you learn what you need to retain procovery, and to recognize early warning signs and cut crises off at the pass.

Who your friends are. In the process of procovery, you learn (and learn to cherish) who your true friends and supporters are.

A renewed sense of self-respect. Because when the going got rough *you* got going, people procovering from chronic mental illness ought to have a renewed respect for themselves, in fact ought to be in awe of themselves and their strength and their courage.

What you can and cannot do. Procovering individuals learn to balance what they cannot do with what is meaningful that they can and want to do. To quote Patricia Deegan, Ph.D., "This is the paradox of recovery, i.e., that in accepting what we cannot do or be, we begin to discover who we can be and what we can do."

A road map to personal meaning. The process of procovery often uncovers passions that can drive a life, from returning to school, to community service, to a renewed spirituality, to advocacy, to a new vocation, to a focus on family and romance.

Attaining Procovery Provides a Road Map to Retaining It

Sometimes despair kills us, or prompts us to kill ourselves. But in throwing us deep inside, despair can also put us in touch with what is left when all else is, or seems, gone. We find the core of who we are, of vitality, a spirit that resists disability, death, and self-destruction.
—James Gordon, M.D.

Procovery is an individualized university from which you have graduated. In short, you know how to stay procovered, because *you did it*.

You know through hard experience the regimen that works best for you, from how to work with supporters and treating professionals, to what self-care techniques work best. You know how and where to best experiment as your body and life change over time. You know the criticality of hope, and of lighting a fire rather than filling a bucket.

You:

- Know that procovery is possible.

- Recognize the power of the individual.

- Focus forward not backward.

- Focus on life rather than illness, and strengths rather than weaknesses, identifying and building on what is available.

- Recognize that big problems don't necessarily need big solutions—value the ordinary.

- Accept backsliding.

- Keep hope alive.

- Just start anywhere.

In retaining procovery, you might:

- Celebrate often how far you've come.

- Shorten the length of visits with treating profession- als rather than the frequency. The natural reaction when procovered is to reduce the frequency of office visits, but addressing issues as they arise is not only a safety measure but also a preventive measure. Staff can also use these opportunities to remind you of the importance of maintaining procovery.

- Do what works, but if it stops working, that's okay. You know from experience that your body may change over time, and there are a multitude of choices (growing daily) of new things to try.

- Create a *base* well-being or wellness plan, the simplest level of things that keep you going. Many days you will choose to take additional steps, but it is important to keep in mind your basic procovery needs. An example might be that you commit to daily: nine hours of sleep; taking medication on schedule; taking a 15-minute walk; 30 minutes of relaxation breathing before bed.

- Seek to surround yourself with hope builders rather than hope busters, where there is a mutual exchange of energy, ideas, and support, and a focus on the possibilities of life.

- Create a procovery scrapbook, with quotes and photos and letters you write to yourself, describing what you've learned, where you've been, where you want to go, reminding you that crises are temporary, life can be beautiful, and you are amazing.

Retaining procovery can also be fueled by remembering what made you want to live during the worst of your suf-

"I don't sing because I am happy. I am happy because I sing"

fering—which can continue to give your life critical meaning now. What pulled you through when life was at its darkest—Love for others? Unlived dreams? Change you want to see in the world? The fuel you used to pull yourself through to procovery can continue to be what fuels you in retaining procovery.

If that doesn't help you answer the question, "What do I

want to do now?" try asking yourself, "In the big picture, what do I want done?" Environmental cleanup? An end to racism? Political change? Increased advocacy on mental health issues? A new business or service? Community building? Increased education on animal rights? Locate others who share your passion. Work toward your shared goal. Now, in any increment. And enjoy. The sky's the limit.

"Ultimately," Victor Frankl wrote, "man should not ask about what the meaning of his life is, but rather he must recognize that it is *he* who is asked. In a word, each man is questioned by life; and he can only answer to life by *answering for* his own life."

Just start anywhere!

Great mother of big apples, it is a pretty world.
—Kenneth Patcher

Acknowledgements

This book could not have been written without the enormous and far-reaching support given to me by my incredibly wonderful, walks-on-water husband, Randy Stratt. Juggling his own demanding career, he served as researcher and editor, as well as coordinated the book production. He helped me develop procovery concepts and strategies and speeches and training, was available to brainstorm at the drop of a hat, and not once did his belief in procovery, or me, waiver. If prior to meeting Randy I had defined my "dream man," he wouldn't have been able to touch the wonder of Randy. Randy has qualities I never knew existed in a man and I thank my lucky stars every day that I get to spend my life with him.

My precious daughters Amanda and Acasia were enormously supportive during my own procovery process and continue to be hugely supportive of my work in procovery. I am in awe of both of them:

Amanda has a positive, contagious energy that I wish I could bottle. She is compassionate and wise and generous and strong. She seemed to have an innate understanding of the procovery process even though she was so very young when I first became ill. She "mothered" Acasia, doted on me and somehow, magically, held on to the most appealing child-like wonder and sense of joy while at the same time developing a fierce determination and strength. Acasia has a knack for getting others to slow down to the speed of life and to enjoy. She has always known the importance of the "little things" in life. When she was only three and I was packing to go in to the hospital she offered for me to take "Tillie" with me, her tiny cloth doll that she had never spent the night without. From cups of tea to homemade pie to painting my toenails and "cracking" my fingers she has blessed my life with her ability to make magic everyday.

My mother, Peggy Crowley, was beside me every step of the way on my path to procovery. When I was overwhelmed on my return home from three months in a psych ward and couldn't for the life of me figure out where or how to begin to put my life back together, she taught me to Just Start Anywhere. She explored with me every possible avenue to procovery. When we hit a dead-end (which we often did) she inspired me to try another route. And most important she has made me feel loved every day of my life.

Until I met Sinikka McCabe I had no hope for improvement of service in the public mental health system and my goal was to stay as far away from it as possible. It was my husband that first met Sinikka and he was so impressed with her he urged me to meet with her. I did so hesitantly. Very hesitantly. But Sinikka's integrity, intelligence and determination to improve services, as well as her engaging personality, melted my heart and redirected my energy.

It was Sinikka who introduced me to William Anthony, via his inspiring article—*Recovery From Mental Illness: The Guiding Vision of the Mental Health Service System in the 1990s* (Psychosocial Rehabilitation Journal, 16, p. 11-23). Bill Anthony is a brilliant and a kind man, who I have had the good fortune to encounter not only through his work but also in person. His remarkable vision, insight and leadership will unquestionably stand the test of time, and will continue to be a major influence in defining how we should understand and treat mental illness. I am honored that he agreed to write the foreword for this book, and I am grateful for his support of *The Day Room* and my activities surrounding procovery. The world seems kinder to me, and far more hopeful, knowing of the work he and the others on the staff at the Center for Psychiatric Rehabilitation are doing.

Chris Hendrickson, Director of the Bureau of Community Mental Health for the State of Wisconsin, for whom I have much affection, whose patience and long-time support for this book and procovery is much appreciated.

Kathleen Eilers, Administrator of the Milwaukee County Mental Health Division, for her vision of and support of procovery, and patience regarding the production of this book.

The wonderful Kaseman family—Larry, Susan, Beth, Peter, Gretchen and Megan. They have been supportive of my work on procovery from the beginning. How our family cherishes their friendship and now that we've moved how we miss getting together with them!

Larry Schomer and I have worked together in a variety of ways. His sensitivity and gentleness and knowledge always amaze me. And he always makes me laugh (and, as they say, he who laughs, lasts).

Lee Jones, M.D., who helped me to procover and helps others learn to do so everyday. Lee is a gift to the medical profession. One of the many things I love that Lee does is teach empathy to students at UCSF.

William Flynn, M.D., astonishes me by continually coming up with new, improved strategies for helping individuals to procover. His insights into procovery and the elderly population are exceptional.

Priscilla Henkelman, who I felt an immediate connection with, has been extremely supportive of procovery and I look forward to working with her more in the future.

Ken Robbins, whose warmth and gentleness I miss now that I no longer live in Wisconsin, and whose early and continued support of *The Day Room*, the Health Action Network, and procovery are much appreciated.

My father, Ernie Crowley, who critiqued this book with a fine-toothed comb and as a former newsman, with a special eye toward whether I was fair to the media in the stigma chapter. He also instilled in me the belief that I am "the world's greatest authority" on me. This proved to be hugely important during my own procovery process when teams of "experts" were often giving me a very different message.

Sally Raschick—who gave me insight and inspiration as to what procovery can mean to the elderly population (and to Brownie Raschick in memoriam).

Lisa Schulz of Elysium Design in San Francisco, the talented and highly professional designer of the jacket cover and book (and website), who donated her services to further procovery and whose design enabled the "just start anywhere" premise of the book. Thank you, Lisa, for your flexibility and creativity and generosity!

Evan Elliot, who made this a better book through his insightful, productive and high-level critique of the manuscript.

Heather Graham, who I met at the very end of the writing of this book and at just the right time. Her inclusions in the feelings chapter have made this a much better book.

Jim Crowley, my big brother, amazes me. He knows more about how to live a life than most anyone I know. I bet he and his wife, Joy, could write a book on procovery that would melt hearts.

Cindy Cotter my sister. She has to have one of the most unusual minds on this earth balanced by a gift for expressing herself that is rare.

Heather Rogalski, whose patience and professional editing and insights were very much appreciated.

Betty Blaska (in memoriam), who made the most wonderful tiramisu I have ever eaten, whose teaching of religion to children made my heart sing, who made for me the most beautiful book of quotes, and who wrote about mental health issues with brilliance and integrity.

Tammy Marshall, whose elegance, gentleness, sunny disposition, and off-the-wall sense of humor I admire and enjoy.

Like procovery itself, this book was not done alone but with the assistance and/or friendship of many others. In addition, I have drawn inspiration from a variety of people, some of whom I have never met! To name just a few (in alphabetical order): Dylan Abraham, Roger Backes, Marion Becker, Amy M. Beyers, Barry Blackwell, Tracy Boldt, Judi Chamberlin, Susan Connors, Laurie Curtis, Wira Daniels, Patricia Deegan, Chris Ellis, Daniel Fischer, Paula Fries, Barbara Gavin, Fran Greene, Dianne Greenley, Susan Hastings, Sally Haveman, Ellen Healion, Carla Itkin, Ann Jennings, Phil and Marylou Johnson (our wonderful next door neighbors in Madison—I miss Wednesday night cards and Lane Bakery cakes!), Andrew Karatsoni, Gerilyn Karatsonyi, Carolyn Kniffen, Ed Knight, Judy Leaver, David LeCount, Tom Leibfred, Rob Marblestone, Mary Moran, Mary Noordhof, Kellianne O'Brien, Bruce Oppenheim, Lorraine Pagliaro, Darbey Penney, Russell Pierce, Richard Raisler, Jason Reiband, Karen Robison, Joseph Rogers, Gilberto Romero, Steven Rosenblatt, Harvey Rosenthal, Jane Schomburg, Bernie Siegel, Jody Silver, Brad Smith (in memoriam), Sharai Smith, Richard Stratt, Benita Walker, Victoria Wilcox, Damien Wilson, Sharee Woessner, Charley Yarley, Mary Rose Yarley.

Index

Index

More Procovery—Contribute Your Stories!

Have you procovered? Have you helped someone else procover? Do you have insights into the procovery process?
Please share your stories and help others learn about the
power of procovery.

Stories may be up to 1500 words (stories may be edited
for clarity and length) and will be eligible for publication
at www.procovery.com and in any future editions of this
and other procovery publications.

Submit to:

> www.procovery.com

> or by mail to:
> The Power of Procovery
> P.O. Box 2247
> San Francisco, CA 94126

Please note that there will be no payment for submis-
sions. And we must be able to get in touch with you if
needed—so PLEASE include contact information (email,
snail mail, phone or fax)!

Kathleen Crowley

Kathleen Crowley is available for keynote speaking, consulting and training. **The Power of Procovery** *and* **The Day Room, A Memoir of Madness and Mending** *can be purchased in quantity at a discounted rate for organizational and fundraising purposes. Please inquire to the below address or email:*

The Power of Procovery
P.O. Box 2247
San Francisco, CA 94126

kcrowley@procovery.com